ECONOMICS

ECONOMICS
A PRIMER

SIMON HAYLEY
ALEC CHRYSTAL

OXFORD
UNIVERSITY PRESS

OXFORD
UNIVERSITY PRESS

Great Clarendon Street, Oxford, OX2 6DP,
United Kingdom

Oxford University Press is a department of the University of Oxford.
It furthers the University's objective of excellence in research, scholarship,
and education by publishing worldwide. Oxford is a registered trade mark of
Oxford University Press in the UK and in certain other countries

Published in the United States of America by Oxford University Press
198 Madison Avenue, New York, NY 10016, United States of America

British Library Cataloguing in Publication Data

Data available

Library of Congress Control Number: 2017954177

ISBN 978–0–19–878705–1

Printed in Great Britain by
Bell & Bain Ltd., Glasgow

PREFACE

This book is aimed at readers with no prior knowledge of economics who need a rapid introduction to the subject. It has evolved out of necessity. Every year students arrive at Cass to start MSc courses in business and finance-related subjects. All have a degree, but some have never studied economics before. We face a tough challenge: during the busy two-week induction period we have just three lectures in which to teach these students the economics they need for their subsequent courses. How much economics can we teach in just a few hours?

The answer, we discovered, is quite a lot—more than we would previously have believed possible. Economics courses are sometimes quite mathematical, requiring students to grind through algebra or complex charts. We found most of this unnecessary. Economics seeks to explain how people behave as consumers, employees, and entrepreneurs— behaviour which seldom involves serious maths. Economics explains intuitive behaviour, so economics itself should be intuitive.

We have had three advantages in developing our material. The first is that we could experiment: our teaching evolved as we repeated these lectures each year and discovered what worked and what did not. Second, we have drawn on our experience in our previous careers in public policy and the private sector, and focussed on the topics that we found to be of most use in real applications. Finally, we have drawn on Alec's experience as co-author of one of the main economics textbooks.

Student feedback was enthusiastic, so we have now converted these lectures into book form and have added some extra material on new topics. You may need to learn economics quickly to meet the demands of a new job, or a course you are about to undertake. Perhaps you just seek a better understanding of economics in current affairs. Whatever your need, we hope you find these lectures as useful as our students have and that we can share what we love about economics: that it helps us understand many of the choices that people make in their everyday lives and many of the issues that are in the headlines every day.

Simon Hayley
Alec Chrystal
Cass Business School, London

CONTENTS

PART ONE: MICROECONOMICS

PART TWO: MACROECONOMICS

CONTENTS

DETAILED CONTENTS

PART ONE: MICROECONOMICS

LIST OF FIGURES

LIST OF TABLES

LIST OF BOXES

CHAPTER 1

INTRODUCTION: OUR ASTONISHING ECONOMIES

We generally take it for granted that most goods are available in shops or online when we need them, but if we step back for a moment, this is rather surprising.

Imagine that you are responsible for running the economy of the country in which you live. To see what an immense task this is, let us consider just a small part of it: shoes. You need to plan how many shoes to produce. How much nylon will you need for the shoelaces and how much rubber for the soles? How many cattle will you need to make the leather? How many farmers will this need? How many vets? What resources will you need to train the vets?

We have only just started! You need to plan the different sizes and styles of shoes that are required and the transport for getting them into the shops where they will be needed. Shoes are only a small part of the economy. Think about the huge variety of different goods that is available when you go into a single shop, let alone a large shopping centre. If you are running this economy you will be responsible for all the decisions that are needed to produce these goods. You will need to coordinate the different jobs that people need to do and the many ways that they interact in order to get this amazing variety of goods into the shops. **Goods** are just the start—there are many **services** to provide as well.

This is a daunting task. It suggests that you need to construct a very detailed plan which can take account of the huge number of interactions that is involved. Without such a plan it seems inevitable that the economy will be a chaotic shambles. Even small planning mistakes will result in wasteful excess production of some goods, whilst shoppers looking for other goods face empty shelves and factories stand idle when they lack vital raw materials or skilled staff.

Against this background, here is the single most astonishing fact about the economies we live in: our governments generally do not make such a plan. Indeed, the history of the twentieth century tells us that economies generally work better if nobody even tries to make such a plan. Some countries did have a Ministry of Planning which made all the major production decisions in the economy. The Soviet Union was one example, and its economy was not able to keep up with what Western economies were able to produce.

The alternative to a **centrally planned economy** is a **market economy** in which individuals and firms make their own decisions, interacting with others in markets. When they produce things they sell them in a market and when they need things they buy them in a market. These markets can take many forms, including shops, street markets, and online auctions. Markets allow economies to function without a central plan.

Let's try a thought experiment. Imagine taking a single country and arbitrarily cutting it in half, leaving similar people and natural resources in each part. Now we run one part as a centrally planned economy and the other as a free market economy with no central plan. What would these two economies look like after fifty years?

Astonishingly, this is not a thought experiment—it actually happened. In fact it has happened at least twice. Once was in Germany, which was divided into East and West following World War II. One major problem faced by the East German government before its collapse in 1989–90 was that its citizens could see from West German TV broadcasts that their own centrally planned economy was clearly delivering living standards substantially lower than in West Germany's market economy.

It also happened in Korea, which was divided in the 1950s at the end of the Korean War. South Korea, a market economy, became one of the 'Asian tigers' with massive economic growth which has completely transformed living standards. By contrast, North Korea's planned economy is a disastrous failure. It generates average living standards far below those seen in the South and has even suffered famine.

Market economies are largely self-organizing. People make their own decisions, generally acting in their own self-interest, rather than thinking about what is best for the economy. Yet when their decisions respond to prices set in open markets the result is a fairly efficient coordination of economic activity. Markets can be thought of as a mechanism which allows consumers and producers to communicate with each other: consumers tell producers what they want and producers tell consumers what is available. This allows them to coordinate their decisions.

Markets economies generally work better than planned economies, but not always. In Chapters 4–5 we will look at situations in which specific markets cannot be expected to work effectively. This will lead us into interesting economic policy issues concerning how the government might wish to intervene to help these markets work better. Similarly, in Part Two we will look at potential economy-wide problems of inflation, recession, and unemployment. But first we will explore how it is even possible that economies can work, and generally work fairly well, even though nobody is making a detailed plan.

PART ONE
MICROECONOMICS

Economics splits naturally into two parts. Microeconomics seeks to explain individual behaviour, such as why consumers and firms make the decisions that they do, and how markets for specific goods and services work. Macroeconomics, by contrast, seeks to explain the 'big picture' phenomena which only make sense when we look at the economy as a whole, such as recessions, unemployment, and inflation. Part One of this book covers microeconomics. We turn to macroeconomics in Part Two.

We start by exploring how consumers and producers interact in markets, and how this process makes it possible for a market economy to function without a central plan. Subsequent chapters explore the possible imperfections of market economies. Chapter 3 examines the behaviour of firms—some of it benign, some less desirable. Chapter 4 identifies specific situations in which markets cannot be expected to work well and government intervention might help. Chapter 5 considers the labour and financial markets (which have distinct features and problems of their own) and wider psychological factors which may affect consumer and firm behaviour.

CHAPTER 2
DEMAND AND SUPPLY

Starting a book on an unfamiliar subject can be daunting, so here is some good news: you are already very good at making economic decisions. We have all spent a lot of time shopping and we can draw on that experience. We don't need to explain how to make these decisions—all we need to do is identify the factors that underlie the decisions we already make by intuition.

Markets take many forms, but what they all have in common is that they bring together two groups of people. One group has money but wants goods and services. These people have **demand**. Most of the time we take this role as consumers. The other group is firms and individuals who **supply** products in return for money.

Our first task will be to analyse the behaviour of consumers and see what determines their demand for a particular product. We then consider the corresponding factors that affect supply. Finally we will consider what happens when these two groups come together in a market.

Consumer Demand

We start by considering the main determinants of demand for a particular good or service. We are all experienced consumers, so this list is likely to contain few surprises:

- *The price of the product*: our demand is not how much of a product we *want*—it is how much we are willing to buy at a specified price. We will generally be willing to buy more of the product at a low price and less at a higher price.

- *Our income*: a higher income allows us to spend more on everything, although our demand for **inferior goods** may fall as we choose higher-quality alternatives instead (we might start to eat fewer sausages and more fillet steak).

- *The price of related goods*: demand for any good is likely to increase in response to a rise in the price of a **substitute** (if the price of coffee rises we might drink tea

Box 2.1 Economic models

The real world is complex. Our economy contains millions of people with different skills and preferences. To analyse it we need to make some simplifying assumptions. There are plenty of bad jokes about economists making unrealistic assumptions, but if we do not simplify at all then we will not be able to say anything useful about why the economy behaves as it does. All we will be able to say is 'I don't know—it's complex'.

These simplifying assumptions allow us to construct models of economic behaviour. In this book we will typically present these models in the form of simple diagrams which aim to capture key aspects of economic behaviour. These are generalizations—people are diverse and there will always be exceptions. But if we choose our assumptions carefully then our model should be realistic enough to allow us to derive conclusions about why things happen and to make predictions about how the economy might behave if the situation changes.

The need to construct simplified models of the world is not unique to economics. Other branches of science have to do the same. If the assumptions used are inaccurate then the model will be misleading, but if our assumptions accurately represent the key forces that are at work then it should improve our understanding of how the world works. As statistician George Box put it: 'All models are wrong, but some are useful'.

instead). Less commonly we may also find **complementary goods** which have the opposite relationship (e.g. we are less likely to buy a car if the price of petrol has increased).

- *External factors*, such as the weather: the goods we consume in summer tend to differ from those we consume in winter. Demand for some goods shifts dramatically around Christmas.

- *Personal characteristics*, such as the consumer's age, religion, and dependents: our consumption also changes dramatically if we have children. In addition people simply have different tastes, and enjoy different types of goods and services.

We can quantify some of these effects. If a firm raises the price of a product demand will fall, but by how much? It turns out that some products are more sensitive to price changes than others. The **price elasticity** measures this sensitivity. Many factors can affect demand, so to keep things simple we measure this elasticity as the change in demand for a good as its price changes whilst the other factors in our list (including the prices of all other goods) stay unchanged. Specifically, if a 1 per cent increase in the price of a particular product leads to 1 per cent fewer units of this product being bought, we would say it has unit price elasticity. Demand is **elastic** if it falls by more than 1 per cent, **inelastic** if it falls by less than this. 'Elasticity' may seem an odd term, but the intuition is that a price rise puts demand under pressure. If demand is elastic then it will be squeezed much lower, if demand is inelastic it will hardly change.

As we are all experienced consumers, we can probably be fairly confident about the elasticity of a range of different goods. First let us consider food, taking all types together and measuring our demand as the total number of calories we consume. Even if the price of food increases dramatically, our total demand is likely to remain relatively stable. Food is an absolute necessity, and we would prefer to economize on our consumption of other goods rather than go hungry. Thus demand for food has a low price elasticity.

We can define **income elasticity** in exactly the same way. If our incomes rise by 1 per cent does our demand for a particular good rise by exactly 1 per cent, or by more (elastic demand) or less (inelastic demand)? If our income rises, we are likely to spend much of the increase on things other than food, and if our income falls we would aim to maintain our consumption of food by spending less on other goods. Thus demand for food is likely to have a low income elasticity as well as a low price elasticity. This puts food near the bottom left corner in Figure 2.1.

The picture is rather different if we consider a specific type of food such as baked beans. Now the price elasticity is likely to be much higher, since if the price of baked beans increases demand is likely to fall, because there are plenty of substitute foods that we could buy instead. By contrast there is no substitute for food as a whole. This puts baked beans further to the right in our diagram.[1]

We can take this process one stage further by considering demand for a specific brand of baked beans. If the price of this particular brand goes up whilst others do not then we might expect a very large fall in demand because consumers have a range of very similar substitutes (other brands of baked beans) as well as entirely different types of food to choose from. This would suggest an even higher price elasticity for a specific brand. However

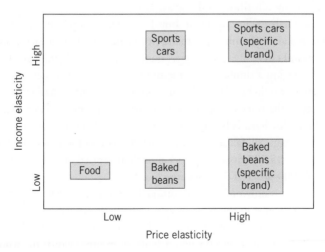

Figure 2.1 Elasticity

this might be partially offset by the effect of brand loyalty. We can regard the marketing expenditure that goes into building up a brand as being designed to convince consumers that this brand is unique: that competing brands of baked beans are not good substitutes. If this marketing effort is successful then the manufacturer can exploit this reduced elasticity by increasing the price of this product without suffering a large drop in demand.[2]

At the other end of the spectrum are luxury goods. We are unlikely to buy these at all if our income is low, but if our incomes rise then a larger proportion of our expenditure might be on such goods. Thus luxuries have a high income elasticity. Sports cars are one example.

The price elasticity of such goods again depends on how narrowly we define them. Demand for a specific manufacturer's cars is likely to have high price elasticity, since if one firm increases its prices consumers can easily switch to another brand.[3] This puts it at the top right of Figure 2.1.

Elasticities are a very practical tool. For example, analysing the price and income elasticities of demand for a product could be a good starting point for constructing a business plan, since it tells us how demand might be affected by a price rise or a recession.

The Demand Curve

We can now dig a little deeper into demand. We saw above that many factors can affect demand for a product, but we will split these into two categories: (i) the price of the good itself, and (ii) everything else (all the other factors we listed in the previous section). As we will see in this section, the price of each good is determined as part of the dynamics of the market, whereas the other factors are not.

Let us consider demand for eggs. We start with a single consumer, Alice. If the price of eggs is very high (£3 per dozen) she buys one dozen per month, but she tells us that she would buy more if the price were lower (2 dozen at £2, 3 dozen at £1). Her demand is elastic, since many substitute foods are available.

Similarly, Bob tells us that he would buy 1½ dozen eggs per month at £3, 2 dozen at £2 and 3 dozen at £1. Summing demand from Alice and Bob at each price gives us a combined **demand curve**: 2½ dozen eggs bought at £3, 4 at £2 and 6 at £1. If we asked everyone in the region a similar set of questions, and added their demands together at each price then we would build up a demand curve for the entire market for eggs (Figure 2.2).[4] A change in the price of eggs moves us from one point on this curve to another. This curve slopes downwards because there are plenty of substitutes for eggs, so if the price rises sales of eggs will fall as consumers switch to other foods instead. For example, demand would be 85,000 dozen eggs per month at a price of £1 per dozen, but this would fall to 70,000 dozen if the price rose to £2.

The price of eggs is only one factor—although an important one—of the many that affect demand. A change in the price of eggs shifts us from one point on the demand curve to another, whereas a shift in one of the other factors would alter the level of demand even if the price of eggs stayed unchanged: in other words the whole demand curve would shift to the left or right. We call this a **demand shock**.

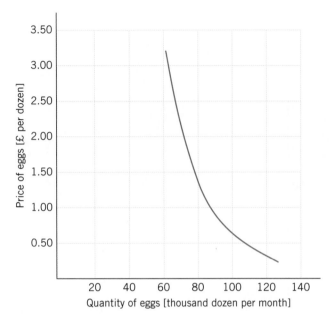

Figure 2.2 Demand curve for the egg market

A positive demand shock might be caused by a rise in the price of a substitute good. For example, if cereals became more expensive, consumers would be more likely to have eggs for breakfast instead. This would shift the whole demand curve for eggs to the right (from D_0 to D_1 in Figure 2.3), since at any given price demand for eggs is now higher than before. For example, at £2 per dozen demand used to be 70,000 dozen, but at the same price it is now 90,000 dozen. The other factors in our list above can have similar effects. For example, rising incomes may also increase demand (to the extent that eggs have a positive income elasticity), as might an advertising campaign by egg producers.

Conversely a reduction in the price of substitutes would tend to shift the demand curve to the left, with consumers buying fewer eggs at any given price. Another example of such a negative demand shock came in 1988 when the UK Minister of Health made an offhand comment about eggs being infected with salmonella. Demand collapsed as nervous consumers decided that they would prefer to buy other types of food instead!

The Supply Curve

We noted earlier that a market is where people with demand (those who have cash they are willing to exchange for goods) meet suppliers (who have goods and services they are willing to sell). So alongside our demand curve we need a corresponding **supply curve** which tells us the quantity that suppliers are willing to sell at each price.

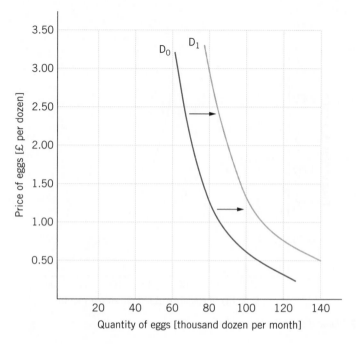

Figure 2.3 A positive demand shock

The most obvious factor affecting supply is again the price of the product. If prices are low then low profit margins mean that suppliers will only be willing to sell a small amount. They will be willing to sell a much larger amount if the price is high—their profit margins will be greater and this is likely to make it worthwhile to expand production even if, for example, the need to pay overtime to their staff increases the average cost of producing each unit. In the longer term high prices might also encourage producers to invest in expanding their production capacity.

As the price of a good increases, demand tends to fall (consumers buy less), but supply tends to rise (producers want to sell more). Thus demand curves slope down, but supply curves slope up.

Other factors can also affect the quantity supplied, such as the price of the raw materials. For example, the price of oil and metals will be important to manufacturers of some goods, whilst the price of chicken feed will be important to egg producers. Increased feed prices would squeeze profit margins and reduce the amount that suppliers are willing to produce. Conversely, falling raw material prices or improvements in technology would have the opposite effect, reducing unit costs and boosting the amount supplied. These other effects can be important, but in drawing a supply curve we make the same distinction as for demand: a supply curve describes how the amount that suppliers wish to sell varies when the price of the good changes whilst all the other relevant factors stay the same. If the price of the product changes, but none of these

Box 2.2 Museum charges

A demand curve is a simple and very useful concept. It tells us the quantity that consumers are willing to buy at different prices, whilst all the other factors that affect demand remain unchanged. In practice these other factors seldom stay unchanged for long, so estimating exactly where the demand curve lies can require complex statistical techniques. However, the UK government gave us a neat example in the 1990s when it decided that some of the major London museums would no longer charge admission fees. The Victoria and Albert Museum had attracted 43,000 visitors per year when it charged £5, but when this fee was abolished it attracted 174,000 (Figure 2.4). Nothing else significant had changed, so this gives us two points on the demand curve, with other points lying somewhere in between.

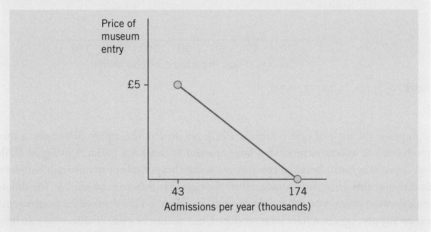

Figure 2.4 Demand for museum admissions

other factors do, we move from one point on the supply curve to another. If instead one of these other factors changes, then the whole relationship between price and quantity supplied is altered. Such a **supply shock** can shift the whole supply curve to the left, as shown in Figure 2.5 (for example, if raw materials become more expensive) or to the right (for example, if cheaper raw materials or improved technology make production cheaper).[5]

Market Dynamics: Supply Meets Demand

We have derived a supply curve and a demand curve. When we combine these we can see how the market works.

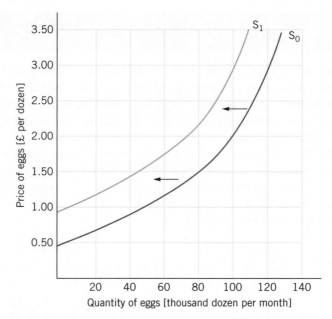

Figure 2.5 Supply in the egg market

Suppose the price of eggs is initially £2.50 per dozen. The supply curve tells us that producers are willing to produce a large amount at this price (point A in Figure 2.6), but demand is much lower, as consumers choose cheaper substitutes instead. Suppliers find that at this price they cannot sell all the eggs that they have produced. The difference between point A on the supply curve and point A′ on the demand curve represents **excess supply**: eggs that have been produced, but cannot be sold. Producers face an ugly choice: either cut the price of these eggs dramatically in order to sell as many as possible, or simply leave them to rot unsold.

Producers won't want to make the same mistake again. Based on what they have just seen they will expect lower prices in future. If they now anticipate a price of £2 per dozen then they will choose to produce a smaller quantity than before (shown by point B on the supply curve). When they take their eggs to market they again find that there is excess supply, although not as severe as before (the gap B–B′ is smaller). Once again, this costly mistake leads them to expect lower prices in future. Every time producers see excess supply, they will expect prices to fall further, and will reduce their production in response.[6]

Conversely, if prices were initially low producers would feel that it is worthwhile to produce only a few eggs, but when they take them to market they would find that they sell out very rapidly. The gap between points C and C′ represents **excess demand** from consumers who would be willing to buy eggs at this price, but who find the shelves bare after the shops have sold out. Once again it will be clear to producers that they have made a mistake, since they missed out on a lot of potentially profitable sales. They will

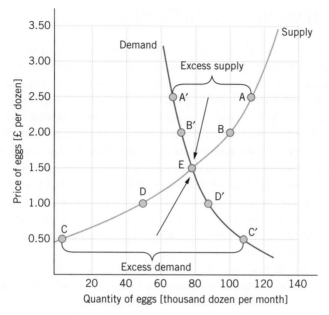

Figure 2.6 Supply and demand in the egg market

expect higher prices in future and will produce more eggs, corresponding to a point higher up the supply curve.

It does not matter whether prices initially start high or low. By a process of experimentation over successive months, producers will learn that a price of £1.50 will avoid both excess supply and excess demand. This leads them to point E, the only point in this chart where the amount that suppliers wish to produce is equal to the amount that consumers wish to buy. Once the industry has arrived at this point, this outcome will be repeated in coming months (so long as there are no other changes affecting producers or consumers).

This process achieves something remarkable. The government is not planning this market. Instead each producer is trying to maximize profits—excess demand and excess supply both represent situations where they failed to do so. As they learn from their mistakes, making their own independent decisions in their own self-interest, we can expect the market to arrive at the point of equilibrium where supply equals demand. This is something that centrally planned economies struggled with—shops in such economies were notorious for having a glut of some goods whilst other goods were unavailable. Writing in the eighteenth century, economist Adam Smith famously likened this to an 'invisible hand', which coordinates economic activity even in the absence of a central plan. It is a remarkable feature of free markets.

However, we should be cautious, since there are circumstances in which markets do not work well without government intervention. We consider these in Chapters 4 and 5.

How Markets Respond to Shocks

Shocks arise when something changes which shifts the demand or supply curve. Figure 2.7 shows a supply shock which might result from an increase in the price of oil or other raw materials. The supply curve shifts up and to the left, since these increased costs mean that only if the price of the good that they produce is higher than before will manufacturers be willing to produce any specified quantity. Following such a shift, we are again likely to see a short period of transition as producers experiment with production levels before the market settles at its new equilibrium B. This new equilibrium is another point on the same demand curve, so we know that compared with the original position A, our new equilibrium involves a lower quantity supplied at a higher price.

Supply shocks can also be good news, such as when manufacturers' costs are reduced by falling raw material prices or—over a longer time scale—by improved production technology. This shifts the supply curve down and to the right and the result is very desirable: a new equilibrium with more output being produced at lower prices.

Let us consider a real example.[7] Figure 2.8 shows that the wholesale price of Brazilian coffee has been volatile, sometimes jumping or falling very rapidly. The jumps were in response to bad harvests which resulted in lower supply than in previous years. Prices responded sharply to news of such bad harvests. For example, in 1994 the price rose from around $1.80 per kg to $4.90.

A bad harvest meant that less coffee was available, so prices had to rise far enough for some customers to decide that they would do without coffee and opt for a substitute such as tea or cocoa instead. When enough customers had switched to alternatives, total demand had been reduced so that it was equal to the reduced supply. In this way the price

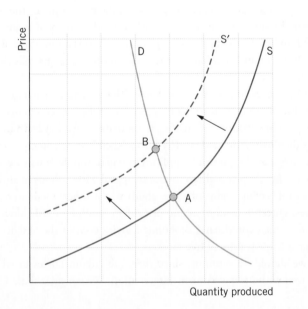

Figure 2.7 Market response to a supply shock

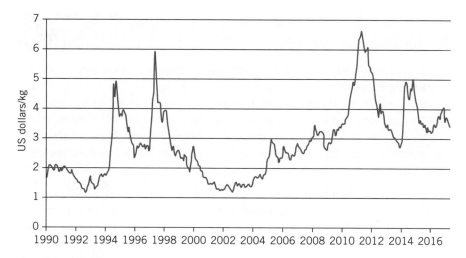

Figure 2.8 Price of coffee
Source: The World Bank Commodity Price Data (the Pink Sheet) online database (Arabica coffee)

rise acted as a rationing mechanism that determined which consumers would continue to drink coffee, and which would choose to spend their money on something else instead.[8]

The very large jumps seen in coffee prices also tell us that demand for coffee is price inelastic, since a large price increase is needed to encourage consumers to switch to other beverages. This means that the demand curve is steep, as shown in Figure 2.7. By contrast, goods with elastic demand have demand curves which slope down more gently

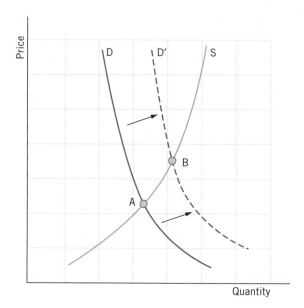

Figure 2.9 Market response to a demand shock

Box 2.3 Scarcity and opportunity cost

Our economic decisions are most interesting when they concern resources that are **scarce**. Air is plentiful—we can continue to breathe as much air as we like (even if the quality is sometimes not what we would wish). By contrast, our income is scarce, so choosing to spend more on one product requires us to spend less on something else. Similarly, in the economy as a whole some resources (such as land, labour, and natural resources) are scarce. Devoting more of these resources to one activity leaves less for others.

As a very simple illustration, Figure 2.10 divides the output of the economy into two categories: the amount of **public sector** output produced in this economy (such as education and health services) is shown on one axis and the amount of all **private sector** goods on the other. We could equally well split the economy in other ways, such as output of cars versus output of all other goods and services. The curved line shows that we can choose to produce a large amount of one type of output and none of the other, or some combination of the two.

If our economy is producing the amounts shown at point A, it is not working efficiently. Resources may be lying idle, or our production processes may not be transforming these resources into useful output as efficiently as they could. Engineers might be able to tell us how to change our processes so as to produce more of both types of output. This might move us to a point such as B which lies on the curve. But we now face a tougher choice. Using more of our scarce resources to produce one type of product imposes an

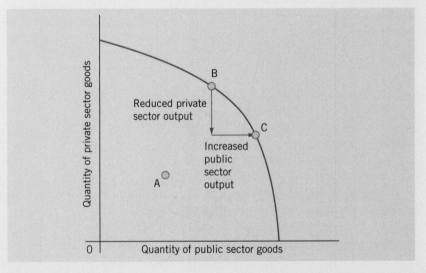

Figure 2.10 Opportunity cost

> **opportunity cost**: the quantity of other goods that we would have to do without. For example we could move from point B to point C, increasing public sector output, but at the opportunity cost of a loss of private sector output. Would such a shift make people be better off? This may be a difficult decision, but it is in this type of decision that economics is most useful, both when we consider our choices as individuals (how to spend our limited incomes) and the use of scarce resources in the economy as a whole. Indeed a good definition of microeconomics is that it studies the *allocation of scarce resources between alternative uses*.

from left to right, and even a small increase in prices would result in many consumers shifting to substitute products, thus removing any excess demand.

Figure 2.9 shows a positive demand shock. The demand curve shifts to the right, but the supply curve remains unchanged. This implies a new equilibrium with more output produced, but at a higher price. The global copper market gives an example of this. Since the start of this century there has been a massive increase in Chinese demand for copper. Over periods of even a few years, the supply of copper is relatively inelastic (even when additional supply can be located it takes many years to open a new mine). This resulted in a large price increase. The market adapted to the increase in demand with some increase in supply, but higher prices also encouraged existing customers to use other products. Thus both supply and demand adjusted to remove excess demand. One noticeable result has been that plastic water pipes are now more common, as builders abandon expensive copper pipes.

Summary

In this chapter we derived a framework for analysing supply and demand for a specified good or service. The quantity demanded is likely to fall as its price rises. It may fall a lot if there are good substitutes available (elastic demand), or very little if there are no close substitutes (inelastic demand). This elasticity determines the slope of the demand curve. Analysing the elasticity of demand is likely to be very useful to firms in choosing their pricing and marketing strategies.

Demand can also be affected by many other factors. These can cause demand shocks which shift the whole curve. Similarly, supply shocks can shift the whole supply curve. Following such shocks producers tend to react to excess supply or excess demand in ways which shift the market back towards the equilibrium where supply equals demand. This is something that planned economies found hard to achieve. Analysis of supply and demand elasticities allows us to predict how prices and quantities will adjust following such shocks.

CHAPTER 3
CONSUMER AND PRODUCER DECISION-MAKING

In this chapter we dig a little deeper into consumer behaviour and then move on to analyse the decisions made by firms. This will lead us to some important policy issues, since whilst much of what firms do is entirely welcome, we can identify some types of behaviour which governments generally aim to prevent.

This may seem a daunting assignment, so let's start with some good news: we can generally regard consumers and producers as facing similar problems:

- Consumers try to make themselves as happy as possible (they maximize their **utility**), constrained by their limited incomes;

- Firms try to maximize their profits, constrained by their costs and the limited demand for their products.

Once again we can use the fact that we are already very experienced consumers. To understand the decisions made by consumers and firms consider a situation that we are probably all familiar with: standing in a supermarket wondering whether to buy one more of one item or an extra unit of something else instead. At this moment we are not considering the entire contents of our shopping basket, we are considering a little bit more or a little bit less of some items. This is known as decision-making **at the margin**.

Consumer Surplus and Decision-Making at the Margin

Let's start with a simple example. Figure 3.1 shows the amount that I would be willing to pay for each successive glass of milk that I consume this week. I put a high value on my first glass. I like the taste and I know it's good for my bones. I would be willing to pay £3 for this glass, but luckily for me the price is only 30 pence. I value my second glass rather less, since I have already met some of my calcium needs, and the second glass is never as enjoyable as the first. The most I would be willing to pay for the second glass is £1.30, but again I'm happy to consume it since it only costs me 30 pence. I enjoy

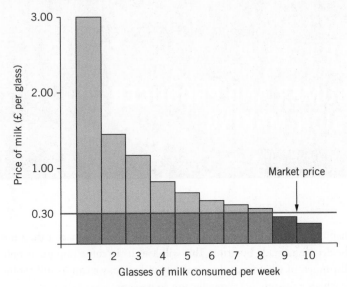

Figure 3.1 Consumer surplus for an individual

further glasses of milk less and less. Indeed, at some point I would become so sick of milk that I would not want to drink more even if it was free!

This illustrates the principle of **diminishing marginal utility**. By utility we mean enjoyment, and marginal refers to the enjoyment I get from consuming one extra unit. The value I put on the eighth glass is slightly greater than the market price, so I will consume it. I will not consume a ninth glass, since I value it less than the 30p it will cost me. Diminishing marginal utility explains why demand for a product increases as the price falls. If milk costs 30p per glass I will stop consuming after the eighth, but if the price falls to 20p, then I will enjoy a ninth glass enough to make this extra purchase worthwhile. Conversely if the price rose to 35p, I would consume only seven glasses, since the eighth is not worthwhile.

I generally don't care very strongly about my final glass of milk, since the **marginal utility** it gives me is worth only slightly more than what I have to pay for it. But I am far from indifferent to the fact that I have been able to drink my first glass. I would have been willing to pay £3 for it, but I only had to pay 30p. This gave me a **consumer surplus** of £2.70 on this purchase. I gained a smaller, but still significant, consumer surplus on my second glass and on every successive glass up to the eighth. If I had not been able to get hold of any milk this week, then my total utility would have been substantially lower because of the large overall consumer surplus that I would have forgone—the total light blue area in Figure 3.1.[1]

Almost all goods we consume give us diminishing marginal utility. We crave variety and become tired of consuming the same things. Furthermore, some goods have a variety of uses, and we put successive units that we buy to less and less important purposes.

Our consumption of water is a good example of this. Drinking at least a bare minimum each day is vital—this keeps us alive. Obtaining more water allows us to do less vital, but still important, tasks such as washing and cooking food. Even more allows us to undertake less important tasks such as washing our clothes, washing our cars, or watering our gardens. Many of us are blessed with extremely cheap and plentiful supplies of water, so we carry on consuming it for progressively more frivolous purposes. The marginal utility we get from the last unit we use is tiny, and the price we pay for this water is equally tiny. But the total utility we get from consuming water is massive because the utility we obtain from more important uses of water (in particular, satisfying our thirst) is so large. Cheap water gives us massive consumer surplus.

Consumer surplus also helps us understand the behaviour of producers. Figure 3.1 shows the consumer surplus for one individual consumer. Figure 3.2a shows the total consumer surplus gained by all consumers in a particular market. For simplicity, let us consider a market in which each person consumes only one unit, such as a ticket to a specific concert. There are some consumers (on the left of the diagram) who would be willing to pay more than £100 for a ticket. Luckily for them the price is only £30, so they make a large consumer surplus. They consider themselves lucky to have had the opportunity to buy a ticket. Other consumers are less enthusiastic: 5000 tickets are sold and to the right of this point the diagram shows people who would value a ticket at less than the £30 market price, and hence choose not to buy one. The total benefit to consumers from the existence of this market is the total consumer surplus (the total difference between what they would have been willing to pay for their tickets and what they actually did pay).

The concert promoter wants to maximize the total revenue generated by ticket sales (for simplicity let us assume that the cost of staging the concert is not affected by the number of people in the audience, so that higher revenue translates directly into higher profits). Total revenue is represented by the rectangle at the bottom of Figure 3.2a. The

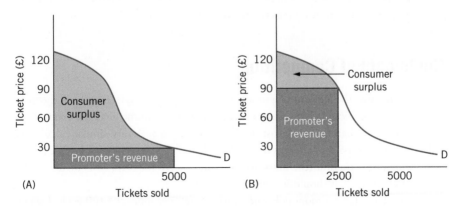

Figure 3.2a Total consumer surplus b Total consumer surplus under monopoly

area of this rectangle is the number of tickets sold multiplied by the ticket price (5000 tickets at £30 each).

However, charging £30 per ticket does not maximize profits. Instead, the promoter would like to capture some of the consumer surplus. Figure 3.2b shows that raising the price to £90 generates greater revenue even though fewer tickets are sold (revenue is 2500 × £90, i.e. £225,000 compared to the previous £150,000). This is because demand for these tickets is inelastic—the price was trebled but demand fell by only 50 per cent. If instead demand had been elastic then trebling the ticket price would have resulted in less than one third of the tickets being sold, thus reducing total revenue. This shows how important it is for producers to understand the elasticity of demand for their products.

Charging the higher price increases profits, but it imposes a large welfare loss on consumers. Consumer surplus has been dramatically reduced to just the small area shown in Figure 3.2b. A large part of the original consumer surplus has now become increased revenue for the promoter as the remaining consumers are forced to pay the higher price. The area to the right of this used to contribute further consumer surplus and additional revenue, but these consumers are not willing to pay the higher price.

This price rise is an example of a **negative sum game** (see Box 3.1). Consumers suffer in two different ways. Some pay the higher price, thus boosting the promoter's profits. Others are priced out of the market, resulting in empty seats at the concert even though they would have been happy to pay at least £30 for them, and would have gained some consumer surplus from doing so.

However, such a dramatic price rise is only likely to be practical if the concert promoter has a **monopoly**.[2] If not, then competitors would make good profits by offering identical concerts at lower prices, so very few tickets could be sold at £90. Knowing that there is competition is likely to deter the promoter from raising prices.

This simple example demonstrates the key problem: the absence of competition allows a **monopolist** to set prices at whatever level maximizes profits, and this can dramatically reduce consumer surplus. For this reason most countries have laws designed to prevent the formation of monopolies wherever possible. Competition means lower profits for producers, but it is far better for consumers.

The Impact of Competition

We saw earlier that the amount of a product that a consumer buys depends on the marginal utility it provides. As long as each successive unit I consume gives me extra utility that I value more than the extra cost, I will consume more. A very similar calculation underlies how much a firm chooses to produce. Will the increase in revenue that results from selling one extra unit (the **marginal revenue**) exceed the extra costs involved (the **marginal cost**)? If so, it should increase production.

Suppose that I have a monopoly and currently sell ten units at £100 each. I know that to sell eleven units I will need to reduce the price slightly since the demand curve

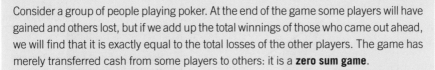

Box 3.1 Zero sum games

Consider a group of people playing poker. At the end of the game some players will have gained and others lost, but if we add up the total winnings of those who came out ahead, we will find that it is exactly equal to the total losses of the other players. The game has merely transferred cash from some players to others: it is a **zero sum game**.

This turns out to be an extremely useful concept as we consider situations in which groups of people interact (these are technically referred to as 'games', although the participants may think of them very differently). Many interactions are **positive sum games**. For example, if the poker players are friends and enjoy their time together then even the players who made modest losses are likely to feel that they have had a pleasant evening. Thus in terms of utility, the game is positive sum, even though in cash terms it is zero sum.

Other interactions are negative sum games. War is probably the most extreme example. The victor might feel that war has been worthwhile in terms of territory or influence gained, but the destruction involved means that the losers will have lost far more than the winner gained. Indeed there are plenty of examples where even the apparent victor is worse off than before. Many forms of crime are negative sum games: they may transfer cash from the victim to the criminal, but at the expense of imposing additional costs on the victim in the form of injury, property damage, and stress, particularly if violence is involved.

Most forms of economic interaction are positive sum games. For example, most markets generate profits for producers whilst also generating consumer surplus (after all, those who feel they are not benefiting should choose not to participate in this market). This is the basic argument behind encouraging **free trade**.

However, we will come across examples of economic interactions which are negative sum games. In such situations the government may wish to intervene to prevent some types of behaviour, effectively changing the rules of the game. The abuse of monopoly power is one example—we will see others in Chapter 4.

slopes downwards. If this new price is £95 I will earn revenue of £1,045 (= 11 × £95), compared to my previous £1,000, so the marginal revenue I earn from producing this extra unit is only £45. The extra unit was sold for £95, but this gain is partly offset by the fact that I had to charge a price on the other ten units that was £5 lower than before (Figure 3.3a).

If producing this extra unit increases my total costs by £30 (the marginal cost) then it would be profitable: my revenue would rise by £45, increasing my profits by £15. In this respect, the decisions made by producers and consumers are very similar. A consumer will consume more milk as long as the marginal utility of an additional glass

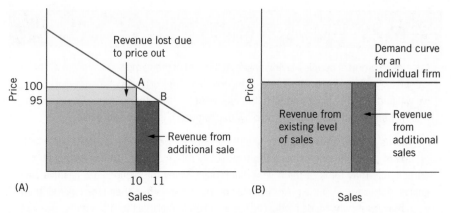

Figure 3.3a A monopolist b A firm in a perfectly competitive industry

is worth more than the additional cost. Similarly, a producer will continue to increase production for as long as the marginal revenue is greater than the marginal cost.

All well and good, but the real benefit of this analysis is that it shows us how competition changes the way firms behave. Instead of a monopoly, suppose that my firm operates in a **perfectly competitive industry** in which a large number of firms sell identical products. Imagine a row of petrol stations along a road—if my station charges even slightly more than the others then I will have no customers, since drivers will all go next door instead. As far as I am concerned the demand curve for my firm is almost perfectly flat (Figure 3.3b).[3] Raising prices is not an option: if I try to charge more than my competitors I will sell nothing. I must simply try to sell as much as I can at the given market price.

By contrast, as the only supplier, a monopolist faces a trade-off. If all customers are offered the same price then the marginal revenue generated by selling extra units will be at least partly offset by having to reduce the price charged on all the sales that the monopolist would make anyway. This greatly reduces the monopolist's incentive to increase sales.

This is the key difference between monopoly and competition. Monopolists restrict the amount they sell and keep the price higher because they know that each extra unit they sell will push down the market price. Firms in **perfect competition** do not restrain themselves in the same way, since they regard their actions as having no impact on the market price. For this reason competitive industries produce more and charge lower prices than a monopoly producer would. Competition results in lower profits for firms, but is much better for consumers, since it avoids the large losses in consumer surplus that we saw in Figure 3.2.

This has important policy implications. It is for exactly this reason that governments generally encourage competition by forbidding firms from (i) merging with their competitors to form a monopoly; (ii) cooperating with their competitors to keep prices high (we consider such behaviour in Chapter 4).

Box 3.2 Are discounts really a bargain?

We have seen that monopolists tend to keep prices high, thus taking a large proportion of the consumer surplus that consumers would have enjoyed at lower prices. We assumed that producers sell all their output at the same price, but what if they can sell identical goods at different prices to different consumers?

Consider a market trader who has no prices marked on his goods—instead he quotes different prices depending on his impression of the potential clients who approach him. He might offer a regular customer a low price, but a wealthy-looking tourist a much higher price. This strategy requires a degree of market power (it won't work if another seller is advertising lower prices next door) and it is risky: some of those who refuse to pay the suggested price may stay and haggle, but others might walk away in disgust. However, a trader who judges his clients accurately could gain substantially at the expense of tourists who pay high prices, whilst also maintaining sales to other consumers who are not willing to pay such prices.

This strategy is known as **price discrimination**. It may seem unfair, but it is probably less undesirable than a monopolist charging a high price to everybody. We saw in Figure 3.2b that those who are not willing to pay this amount are priced out of the market, and so gain no consumer surplus at all. By contrast, charging a high price to some consumers and a lower price to others allows both sets of consumers to continue to enjoy some consumer surplus.

Price discrimination is quite common. For example, train tickets are relatively cheap for customers who buy in advance, whilst identical seats on the same train are sold at much higher prices to those who buy at the last moment.[4] Similarly, retailers may offer lower prices to customers who collect discount coupons. Claiming the discount has to involve some inconvenience for the customer. The firm is hoping that customers who are willing to pay higher prices will not bother to claim the discount (perhaps because they are wealthier or lazier, or because it is their employer who is paying), and so end up paying the full price. This strategy is not perfect: some of those who book ahead would have been willing to pay the full fare, and the firm may lose a few customers who were not willing to pay the full fare, but were not able to book ahead. Nevertheless, price discrimination can significantly increase profits.

Producers naturally describe the lower price as a discount given to favoured customers, but it might be more accurate to describe the higher price as the producer taking advantage of consumers who have accidentally signalled (by failing to book in advance or collect coupons) that they are willing to pay higher prices. Online sales may offer increased scope for price discrimination, since the price offered can be adjusted in response to all the information that the seller has already collected about the buyer.

How Much Competition Is There?

In practice, most industries are likely to lie somewhere in the range between perfect competition and monopoly. Few firms are likely to have a complete monopoly, since governments generally prevent such monopolies from forming. Similarly, few industries are perfectly competitive: different firms' products are seldom absolutely identical, and customers may prefer one company out of brand loyalty, or if competitors are slightly more distant or less convenient.

Perfect competition assumes: (1) that new firms can enter the industry; and (2) that all firms sell identical products. In reality there are lots of industries where the first of these assumptions is true, but the second is not. For example, restaurants and producers of goods such as cars, computers, and smart phones can be brutally competitive and very dynamic as firms compete not just by offering low prices, but also by producing different versions of the product that they hope consumers will prefer. This is known as **monopolistic competition**. Firms which produce the most attractive products might be able to charge slightly higher prices than their competitors, but this advantage may well not last. For this reason, monopolistic competition is generally regarded as benign. What really matters for consumers is that firms are competing and that high profit levels would attract new firms to enter the industry.

More generally, assessing the degree of competition in an industry requires judgement, since:

(1) It is not always clear which firms should be considered part of a particular industry. Different products and brands may not be identical, but we should not conclude that each has a monopoly. How much they are in competition depends on the extent to which consumers regard different firms' products as substitutes. Drivers may regard the petrol sold by different suppliers as identical (perfect substitutes), which was why this example was close to perfect competition. By contrast, nearby restaurants are likely to be only partial substitutes for each other, since they serve different food—few consumers are likely to ignore these differences and always choose the cheapest. Conversely, goods (and services) can be substitutes even if they look very different from each other. For example, only one airline might offer flights between two particular cities, but there may still be competition, since passengers might choose to fly to other nearby cities or travel by train instead. If consumers regard these alternatives as acceptable substitutes then it would be misleading to regard this airline as having a monopoly.

(2) A firm which does not currently face any direct competitors may also be deterred from increasing prices if it fears that this would encourage competitors to enter this profitable market.[5]

(3) Competition depends not only on the number of firms in the industry, but also the extent to which they choose to compete. Firms might instead cooperate in keeping

Table 3.1 Possible market structures

	Perfect competition	Monopolistic competition	Oligopoly[1]	Monopoly
Identical products	√	✗	√	✗
New firms can enter	√	√	✗	✗
Firms compete on price	√	√	?	✗

[1] The defining characteristic of oligopoly is that there are only a few firms in the industry, leaving it unclear how much they will compete on price. Do oligopolists produce identical products? Not necessarily. What we have described in this chapter is the simplest model, which makes it clear why oligopoly is different from perfect competition. If we need to analyse the behaviour of an industry where a few firms produce differentiated products then we will need to use a more complex model which includes features of monopolistic competition and oligopoly. A key judgement in applying economics successfully is selecting an appropriate model—one that captures the key features of reality without being unnecessarily complex (see Box 2.1).

prices high. Such **cartels** are generally illegal, because they disadvantage consumers in exactly the same way that a monopoly does.

(4) Even without explicit cooperation between firms, if there are only a few firms in the industry (an **oligopoly**), they may start acting like a monopolist. For example, if my firm accounts for a substantial proportion of sales in this industry then I know that increasing my output by a significant percentage is likely to reduce the market price. This makes me think like a monopolist, and question whether it is worthwhile pursuing these extra sales, especially if I would expect my competitors to respond with price cuts of their own, triggering a price war. I might decide that it would be better for me to keep my prices high and not rock the boat. Such **tacit collusion** can lead to a situation similar to a cartel.

We now have a range of different models, or **market structures**, which might fit different industries, ranging from perfect competition at one extreme to monopoly at the other (see Table 3.1). These can be used for guiding the thinking of managers in these industries and of policy-makers considering government intervention to protect consumers. Governments seldom choose to intervene as long as firms compete on price, and new firms can enter the industry. By contrast, governments might well choose to intervene in oligopolistic industries, especially if tacit collusion or explicit cartel agreements lead firms to charge high prices.

Summary

In this chapter we saw that the behaviour of consumers and producers is in some ways surprisingly similar, since both make decisions at the margin. Consumers buy more of a product if the marginal utility is worth more than the price charged, thus boosting their total consumer surplus. Similarly, firms increase production if the marginal revenue this generates is greater than the marginal cost, boosting their profits. Our analysis of consumer surplus helps to explain price discrimination.

Firms' behaviour is very sensitive to the degree of competition in the industry. Each firm in a perfectly competitive industry regards its demand curve as flat, so all have a strong incentive to boost sales as much as possible. By contrast, a monopolist is deterred from increasing sales by the knowledge that this will push the market price down.

More generally, monopoly and perfect competition are two ends of a spectrum. Most firms will find themselves somewhere in between. The degree of competition in an industry depends upon (i) the availability of substitutes, (ii) whether there are barriers preventing competitors from entering the industry; (iii) whether firms in the industry are competing or cooperating.

Inadequate competition can result in high prices and a dramatic reduction in consumer surplus, so governments in most countries encourage competition. However, we will see in Chapter 4 that it is not practical to prevent monopoly in some industries. We then identify government policies which can be used to respond to this and other **market failures**.

CHAPTER 4
MARKET FAILURES

We started this book with the astonishing fact that market economies have generally performed better than centrally planned economies. We subsequently saw how consumers and producers respond to shifts in market prices (Adam Smith's 'invisible hand') and how this can generally achieve a fairly efficient use of scarce resources even without any central plan. However markets do not always work well.

For now we continue to assume that consumers and producers act rationally (maximizing their utility and profits, respectively). We will relax this assumption in Chapter 5 when we consider behavioural economics. However, there are situations in which even completely rational behaviour can lead to very undesirable outcomes. In this chapter we identify four such market failures. In each case we will examine the extent to which appropriate government policies can improve the situation.

Natural Monopoly

We saw in Chapter 3 that monopoly power allows firms to raise prices, substantially reducing consumer welfare. For this reason most governments have passed legislation which forbids large companies from combining to form a monopoly (**competition policy**). But in some cases competition is simply not feasible. For example, it would be prohibitively expensive for competing water companies to each run a separate set of pipes to every house. The same is true for electricity and gas supply networks. Where competition is not practical such **natural monopolies** need to be prevented from taking advantage of their monopoly power. In some countries this is achieved by keeping these firms in public ownership (nationalized industries) so that they pursue objectives other than maximizing profits. In others these companies are privately owned, but are regulated by government bodies which impose maximum prices which the firms are allowed to charge. This protects consumers by mimicking the effect of competition.[1]

Information Problems

If consumers are to make sensible decisions they need reliable information about the goods and services that are on offer. In most cases this is not a problem: consumers are the best judges of what will best meet their needs and make them happy. But there are exceptions.

For example if I am buying a new car, I can choose for myself the size, speed, and style that I think best, but I would find it hard to judge whether the car was safe. Safety features tend to be hidden from view and in any case I don't have the specialized knowledge I would need to assess their effectiveness. Worse, safety features cost money, but if consumers cannot see whether one car is safer than another they will tend to choose cheap unsafe cars rather than cars which are safer but more expensive. Producers of safe cars will find few buyers and the roads will be full of unsafe cars.

There are two broad approaches that the government can take to prevent such problems: either (i) forbid the sale of goods or services which fall below a minimum quality standard, or (ii) ensure that consumers are provided with the additional information that they need to make a sensible decision. In either case the government needs to employ specialist inspectors to check that minimum standards are being met and that information is reported accurately to consumers. We can find many examples of governments taking each of these approaches:

- Goods such as electrical products must meet specified safety requirements if they are to be sold within the EU. Appliances such as fridges, freezers, and washing machines must also display information about their power efficiency, allowing consumers to make an informed choice between units that are cheap to buy and those which are initially more expensive, but cheaper to run.

- Similarly, cars must satisfy minimum safety standards and manufacturers are required to publish the fuel economy of each model (estimated on the basis of standardized tests) to give consumers an indication of their likely running costs.

- Many governments employ specialists to inspect hygiene standards in restaurants, and have the power to close down those which do not meet minimum standards.

- Similarly, government specialists assess the trustworthiness of financial institutions (the UK's Financial Conduct Authority), the quality of the teaching in our schools (OFSTED), and the content of films and DVDs (extreme content is forbidden, and labels give information about the level of sex, violence, and profanity in each film).

As this list shows, information problems are widespread. Even governments which are firmly committed to free markets tend to intervene in order to give consumers the information that they need to make good decisions. Online reviews—if trustworthy—can also help in some markets.[2] Nevertheless, information failures can still sometimes cause severe problems. Specifically, they were a major cause of the 2008 global financial crisis (see Chapter 5).

Externalities

Sensible decision-making does not just depend on having adequate information—it also depends on the incentives of decision-makers. In most cases this is no problem since the only person who is affected is the consumer. I buy a sandwich for my lunch and I eat it. No one else is affected and I have every incentive to make a good choice. But if other people are affected, then bad decisions can be made. For example I may choose to buy an old car which is very noisy and has a smelly exhaust. I may be very happy with my purchase, but my neighbours might disagree! This is known as an **externality**—the effect that one person's choice has on other people who were not involved in the decision. This is not a problem if people take the welfare of others into account in making these decisions, but unfortunately this is not something that we can take for granted. If instead people are selfish and take decisions based only on their own welfare (as our discussion of consumer behaviour in Chapters 2 and 3 assumed) then we can end up with decisions which are clearly undesirable for society as a whole.

Firms can also generate large externalities, particularly in the form of pollution. Measures to reduce pollution levels (such as clean production processes and safe disposal techniques) tend to be expensive, so if firms are only interested in maximizing profits they will reject such measures and pollution levels will be high. Again, decisions which are entirely sensible from the point of view of individual firms can lead to outcomes that are very undesirable for society.

Just as for information problems, government intervention to combat externalities can take two forms. The first is simply to forbid certain activities. For example, chloro-fluorocarbons (CFCs) used to be widely used in refrigerators and aerosols, but they were found to damage the Earth's ozone layer. International agreement was reached to phase out the use of CFCs. Similarly, individual governments typically forbid high levels of noise pollution and ineffective vehicle exhausts which emit high levels of particulate pollution.

Instead of an outright ban, the government can try to alter incentives so that an appropriate trade-off can be reached between the costs of reducing an externality, and the benefits that this would bring. One way to do this is to impose an additional tax or charge which converts an externality (which people are likely to ignore) into an incentive that they will not ignore. This is known as **internalizing the externality**.

For example, industrial emissions of carbon dioxide are generally agreed to adversely affect the global environment, but it is seldom practical to demand that firms produce zero emissions. In this situation carbon taxes can internalize the externality by charging a tax for each tonne of carbon dioxide (CO_2) that firms emit. This gives firms an incentive to invest in clean technology which reduces their CO_2 emissions, since instead of being an externality that they can ignore, the carbon tax has a direct impact on their net profits. In principle this should lead to sensible trade-offs being made between the cost of measures to reduce emissions, and the harm generated by the emissions themselves. This requires (i) that firms can be prevented from cheating (by emitting undeclared CO_2); and (ii) that the tax is set at a level which accurately reflects the damage inflicted on the environment by additional CO_2 emissions. There is plenty of scope for debate about whether the level is too high or too low, so the policy may well not be perfect. But it is likely to be much better than doing nothing, which would allow firms to ignore the externality and pollute as much as they like.

I know that I face a slow journey if I choose to drive on roads that are already congested, but the presence of my car on the road also imposes an externality, since it increases the level of congestion suffered by every other road user. Congestion charges aim to internalize this externality by encouraging consumers to consider whether their journeys are important enough to be worth the slight increase in congestion that they will cause. The central London congestion charge is currently set at a standard level of £11.50 per day for driving at peak times. If this accurately represents the additional inconvenience that my journey imposes on other road users, then it should encourage sensible decision-making. If I think that the benefits of using my car today more than outweigh the £11.50 externality that this imposes on other people, then it is sensible for me to drive. If it doesn't, then it is better that I don't. Again, this policy may not be perfect, but it is likely to be much better than doing nothing and accepting high levels of congestion as drivers ignore the externality they cause.

Box 4.1 Information problems or externalities?

Some decisions can be affected by multiple market failures, and it is important to be clear about the rationales involved if we are to find appropriate policies for dealing with them. For example, many countries make it compulsory to wear a seat belt in order to reduce the risk of serious injury in car accidents. This can be controversial. When introduced in the UK in 1983 some regarded it as an unacceptable infringement of liberty by a 'nanny state', arguing that individuals should decide for themselves about the risks that they choose to take. An alternative view is that even with good information about the risks involved, people would still make bad decisions since they would tend to ignore the externalities involved, such as the cost of treating injured drivers at public expense in the National Health Service.

Similar issues arise concerning the consumption of alcohol, tobacco, and recreational drugs. One argument is that people consume too much of these because they are insufficiently aware of the likely effect on their health. Public information campaigns have aimed to raise awareness of these effects, but even well-informed consumers may find it difficult to make sensible decisions if the substance is addictive. This argument suggests more interventionist policies, such as high levels of taxation on alcohol and tobacco, and the criminalization of some drugs. A separate line of argument focuses on externalities, such as: (i) the costs of treating the long-term health effects at public expense; (ii) the effects on other people resulting from public drunkenness and drug use, and the effect on non-smokers of breathing other people's smoke in public places. Imposing high taxes on alcohol and tobacco helps to internalize these externalities.

Public Goods

Our final market failure comes about when goods and services can be jointly consumed by many people. For most goods consumption is exclusive: if I eat my sandwich then you can't eat it. Similarly, we cannot share a haircut. However, there are exceptions, such as parks. I can enjoy a walk in the park whilst other people are doing exactly the same. Sharing this service is not a problem in itself. The problem is how to pay for the upkeep of such facilities. First, it may not be practical to charge users. We could in principle put a fence around a small urban park and charge admission, but that is unlikely to be practical for a national park which covers a large area of countryside.

Furthermore, even if we could charge for using the service, this might be a bad policy. Figure 4.1 shows the demand curve for using a particular park: 1000 people would use it each day if they had to pay £5 admission. This raises revenue that can be used for maintenance, and these users still gain a consumer surplus since the value they put on using the park is greater than the £5 they have to pay. So far, so good. But if we look further to the right we see that there are other potential users who would welcome a trip to the park, but value it at less than £5, and so are deterred by the entry fee. Letting these additional visitors into the park would cost nothing (the park is already there), so it would be wrong to exclude them. Figure 4.1 shows that charging a fee to enter the park dramatically reduces consumer surplus, just like a monopolist does (see Figure 3.2). If the park is becoming congested, then each visitor imposes an externality on other users, so charging a fee (like the congestion charge for motorists) would be sensible. But if the

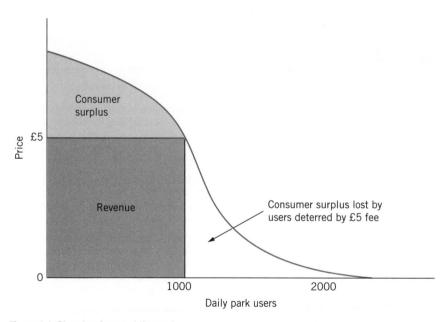

Figure 4.1 Charging for a public good

park is not congested then charging a fee would reduce total consumer surplus by more than the revenue raised.

There are many such **public goods** which are jointly consumed by many users. Broadcast services are another example, since an additional viewer or listener costs nothing. The same applies to our police and justice services, since deterring criminals benefits any number of law-abiding citizens. Road networks are also public goods as long as they are not congested (as we have seen, it makes sense to charge for them if they have become congested).

Public goods can be hugely beneficial. The problem is how to pay for them. Charging users directly is often impractical and undesirable, so governments provide many such services free to users, funded out of general tax revenue. This too is often not an ideal solution since the government's ability to raise tax revenue is limited, implying that some tough decisions must be made in setting priorities for government spending.[3] For this reason charges are sometimes levied (e.g. toll roads and subscription-funded broadcasting services) even for services which could be considered public goods.

We have identified four market failures. These are summarized in Table 4.1, together with possible policies that can address these problems. However, government intervention cannot always be relied upon to correct market failures. The government may not have the information it needs to set the right policies. We might also question whether the government's underlying objective is to set the best policies, or instead to influence voters in order to win the next election (which might lead to very different results).[4] Government intervention might also be affected by lobbying on behalf of interest groups. In practice a perfect solution may not be available—instead we need to weigh the costs of market failure against the possibility of **government failure** which could lead to flawed policies being imposed in response to the market failure.

Table 4.1 Market failures

	Problem	Possible policy responses
Monopoly	High prices result in large loss of consumer surplus	(i) Laws forbidding firms from combining to form monopolies or cooperating in cartels (ii) Where competition is impractical (natural monopolies) nationalize or impose price limits to prevent the firm exploiting its monopoly
Information problems	Consumers cannot distinguish between high- and low-quality goods	(i) Forbid the sale of goods below a minimum quality standard (ii) Provide better information to consumers (e.g. improved labelling)
Externalities	Decisions made by one individual or firm affect other people	(i) Outright ban on the activity which causes the externality (e.g. the production of CFCs) (ii) Internalize the externality by imposing a tax or charge which reflects the costs imposed on other people (e.g. carbon taxes, congestion charge)
Public goods	Not practical or desirable to charge for use	Government funding, although raising the required tax revenue may be a problem

Box 4.2 Asymmetric information and incentives

We have seen in this chapter that consumers sometimes lack the information needed to make good decisions. But the problem can be much worse if the seller has better information about the product than the buyer. Buying a used car is a good example of such **asymmetric information**, since the seller has typically driven the car for some time, and so may be aware of faults that are not immediately apparent to the buyer.

Suppose that you are considering buying a particular car and, based on what you know about it, you estimate that it could be worth £2,000 if there are no hidden faults, but severe faults could mean that the car is actually worthless. With the car worth somewhere between zero and £2,000, you might decide to offer £1,000 for it. But the seller has better information about the car's value, and will refuse your offer if she knows that the car is actually worth more than this. Your offer will only be accepted if the car is worth between zero and £1,000, so you are bound to get a bad deal. Should you offer £500 instead? No—this offer too would only be accepted if the seller knows that the car is worth less than this. In this scenario, asymmetric information results in the complete breakdown of the market: buyers should anticipate that they are bound to end up with a bad deal, and sellers of good-quality cars will not be able to find buyers at an attractive price.

Various measures have evolved to help reduce this problem. You might see used cars advertised with 'genuine reason for sale', implying that these sellers are aware of buyers' concerns, and are claiming that their motive is not simply to get rid of cars that they know are faulty. Unfortunately, this claim may not be credible. Milometers and log books are more effective ways of giving buyers better information. The buyer can also pay to have the car inspected by an independent expert. Finally, a professional used car salesman may offer a warranty which permits the buyer to return a car which turns out to be faulty, although this reassurance is likely to come with a higher price tag.

Asymmetric information is also a serious problem in insurance markets, since those who wish to purchase insurance are likely to have better information about their risk levels than the insurer. For example, health insurers fear that the only people who will buy insurance are those who know that they are particularly high risk. To reduce this **adverse selection**, insurers ask for detailed information about the applicant's current health and lifestyle, and vary their premium in response.

A separate problem is that insurance can alter incentives in ways which systematically increase risk. This **moral hazard** can result in careless driving by those who no longer have to worry about the cost of minor crashes, or even criminal arson of insured buildings. This is why insurers often offer to pay most, but not all, of the costs of an accident, thus ensuring that the insured party still has an incentive to avoid having to claim.

Asymmetric information and incentive problems are also widespread in labour markets, as we shall see in the Chapter 5.

Strategic Games: When Do People Cooperate?

Microeconomics analyses how people are likely to act in their roles as consumers, employees, or managers. Most of the situations we have analysed so far have involved relatively simple behaviour. **Strategic behaviour** is more complex because it considers how we should respond to other people's behaviour and how these other people are likely to respond to our choices. Consider the difference between darts and chess. Darts is a non-strategic game. No matter what your opponent does, your best choice is to score points as quickly as possible. By contrast, playing chess involves anticipating how your opponent is likely to respond to the move you make now. Expert chess players try to think several moves ahead. This is strategic behaviour.

The analysis of strategic behaviour belongs to part of economics called **game theory**, but do not be misled by the name: the 'games' that it analyses refer to strategic interactions between participants with different interests. This includes situations of substantial—sometimes global—importance. Specifically, game theory can help us understand the incentive problems associated with externalities and public goods.

To introduce game theory we need to tell a story:

The prisoner's dilemma

A police patrol catches two men red-handed leaving a house with valuables that they have clearly taken from inside. When the police search the house they find a man dead in an upstairs room. The forensic team quickly establishes that the man was murdered, but they find no fingerprints or other evidence which directly links either of the burglars to the murder. The police know that they do not have enough evidence to convict the men of murder, but the wily old police chief instructs that the men should be interrogated in separate rooms where they will each be told the following:

'What happens next depends on whether you give evidence against the other prisoner. We have enough evidence to convict you for burglary, but if you give evidence linking the other prisoner to the murder we will drop the burglary charge and let you go free. If the other prisoner gives corresponding evidence against you then you will be tried for murder, but even then you would be given a reduced sentence if you gave evidence against the other prisoner. Make your decision now: are you going to give evidence? You will not be allowed to change your mind later.'

To clarify the situation, let us give specific figures for the jail terms that the prisoners should expect. Table 4.2a shows the four possible outcomes for Prisoner A. The top row shows that if Prisoner B stays silent then Prisoner A faces a one-year sentence for burglary if he too stays silent, and no jail term if he gives evidence against B. If Prisoner B does give evidence against A (the second row), then A faces a ten-year jail term for murder, although this will be reduced to five years if A agrees to give evidence against B.

This may seem a rather contrived story, but once we have analysed the behaviour of the prisoners, you will start to recognize exactly this type of situation in everyday life. The story is not intended as a parable about crime and justice or about honour among

Table 4.2a Prisoner's dilemma: Jail term for Prisoner A

	Prisoner A remains silent	Prisoner A gives evidence
Prisoner B remains silent	1	0
Prisoner B gives evidence	10	5

thieves. Instead it is intended to illustrate how the two prisoners might respond to the incentives they have been given. Try to consider it as dispassionately as you would a game of chess. For this exercise you should also assume that neither of the prisoners cares what happens to the other. Indeed, who actually committed the murder is irrelevant: all each prisoner wants is to get out of his current predicament with the shortest possible jail sentence. What should they do to achieve this?

The solution is surprisingly straightforward. The key is that each prisoner is interrogated separately. Imagine that you are Prisoner A, facing the possible jail terms shown in Table 4.2a. You don't know whether the other prisoner is going to give evidence against you, but there is nothing that you can do to affect his choice anyway, so consider the two possibilities in turn. If you assume that the other prisoner is going to remain silent then your choice is between the two options in the first row. If you too stay silent then you will go to prison for one year, but if you give evidence you will go free. Giving evidence is clearly the better option for you.

What if Prisoner B does give evidence against you? If you stay silent then you will end up in the worst possible situation (a ten-year sentence for murder), so here too your best option is to give evidence against the other prisoner. The situation is complex at first sight because your best choice seems to depend on the other prisoner's decision, but in fact it makes no difference. Regardless of whether the other prisoner gives evidence against you or not, your best choice is to give evidence against him.

Table 4.2a showed the prison terms faced by Prisoner A. We can complete the picture by adding the corresponding terms for Prisoner B. These are shown in bold in Table 4.2b. Prisoner B faces the same jail term as A in the top left (where neither prisoner gives evidence) and the bottom right (where both give evidence), but ten years in the top right and zero in the bottom left (since one prisoner goes free only when the other goes to jail for ten years).

Prisoner B has exactly the same incentives as Prisoner A. He does not know whether A will give evidence, but it does not matter, since whether A gives evidence (the right column) or does not (the left column), the outcome for B is better in the bottom row (where B gives evidence) than the corresponding outcome in the top row (B remains silent).

Table 4.2b Prisoner's dilemma: Jail terms for Prisoner A/**Prisoner B**

	Prisoner A remains silent	Prisoner A gives evidence
Prisoner B remains silent	1/**1**	0/**10**
Prisoner B gives evidence	10/**0**	5/**5**

Each of the prisoners can see that his best option is to give evidence against the other. Thus the prisoners end up in the bottom right corner of the diagram—both receive a five-year sentence.

The prisoner's dilemma gives us important insights into when people can be expected to cooperate with each other. Indeed, it leads us to an unexpected conclusion: both prisoners might be aware that they are likely to end up with the uncooperative outcome in which both receive five-year sentences. They might know that they would both be better off if they keep silent. They could even promise each other that they will keep silent. None of this matters, because as soon as they are separated they each have a clear incentive to give evidence against each other. The prisoner's dilemma is a tragedy in which the prisoners are unable to cooperate in order to avoid an obviously undesirable outcome.

Sadly, we see exactly such situations in real life, resulting in uncooperative outcomes which are worse for everybody. As a first example, consider fare dodging on public transport: what will happen if we all know that we can get away with **free riding** rather than paying our fare? This could lead to exactly the same situation as in Table 4.2a. If I assume that other people will pay their fare then the (selfish) best option for me is to free ride, and rely on other people's fares to keep the bus service going. If, instead, I assume that other people won't pay their fares then I would be a fool to be the only one paying. Either way, free riding is the best option for me. But if everybody thinks this way then we will end up in the uncooperative solution in the bottom right of the table: everybody will free ride and the bus service will close down because it has no revenue with which to pay the drivers. The tragedy is that this leaves us with no bus service, even though everybody might have preferred to remain in the top left corner in which we each pay our fare and the bus service continues. Cooperation would make us all better off, but none of us as individuals has any incentive to cooperate.

In order to avoid this, we could change the incentives by employing ticket inspectors who can impose a penalty sufficient to convince us not to free ride. However, there are many other real-life prisoner's dilemma situations in which it is harder to force people to cooperate.

- *Pollution.* We all benefit from an unpolluted environment, but if my contribution to total pollution is fairly small ('my little bit won't make any difference') then my best option is to continue to pollute, thus avoiding the extra cost of cleaner processes and ignoring the externality that my action imposes on other people. When everybody else does the same, we end up with substantial pollution. This logic applies to both large-scale industrial pollution and small-scale individual pollution such as dropping litter or driving a car with a faulty exhaust.

- *'Pirate' music, movies, or software.* The best option for me is to download free copies, whilst relying on other people to pay for their content. But, just like free riding on the bus, if everyone thinks the same, then nobody has any incentive to produce any of this output.

- *Overfishing.* Improved technology such as sonar and refrigeration has made trawlers much more efficient, so fishing fleets can now catch far more fish than is consistent with maintaining adequate stocks in the sea for future years. The need to limit total

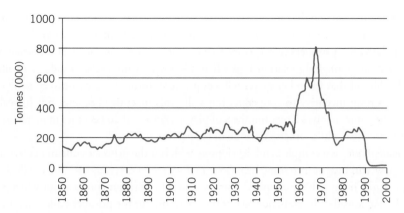

Figure 4.2 Catches of Newfoundland cod
Source: Dr R. Meyers, Canadian Dept of Fisheries and Oceans, St John's, Newfoundland

catches may be obvious, but each individual country involved (and each individual trawler captain) has an incentive to continue to catch large numbers of fish whilst relying on others to cut their catches to sustainable levels. Maintaining fish stocks requires multi-party agreements to limit catches, with effective mechanisms to prevent cheating. The Grand Banks off Newfoundland had been fished for centuries, and used to be famous for the number of cod they contained. As Figure 4.2 shows, in the 1960s improved technology raised the total catch above sustainable levels. Catches initially rose, but then started to fall as stocks plummeted. Fishing cod in this area has been banned since 1992. Stocks are recovering only slowly, and remain well below earlier levels. Failure to cooperate led to the near-destruction of this valuable resource.[5]

In these and many other real-life situations the prisoner's dilemma threatens to leave everybody worse off than if they had cooperated. We have mentioned setting up mechanisms to punish cheats, but there are other ways to encourage cooperation. We can illustrate these by changing the initial scenario slightly.

We assumed that the two prisoners are entirely selfish. If instead they care about each other then they will both stay silent and will end up in the cooperative outcome. This is better for both of them. In this case, altruism brings its own reward. We explore such motives in more depth later (in behavioural economics in Chapter 5, and happiness theory in Chapter 11), but it is clear that people are not always as selfish as our simple model assumed: humans are social animals and the concept of 'fairness' is deep-rooted. Unfortunately, selfish behaviour becomes more likely in larger and more impersonal groups.

Our other key assumption was that each prisoner knows that his own choice has no effect on whether the other prisoner will give evidence. The outcome would be very different if the two prisoners are interrogated together in the same room, since as soon as one prisoner agrees to give evidence the other has an obvious incentive to do the same rather than accept the full ten-year sentence. Cheating is no longer a viable option, since I cannot expect the other prisoner to remain silent whilst I give evidence. We both know this, so there are now only two possible outcomes: the cooperative outcome (top left) where we both remain silent and the outcome where we both give evidence (bottom right). Of these two the cooperative outcome is clearly preferable, so we are both likely to remain silent.

Similarly, the prisoners in our story faced a one-off decision, but real-life situations may instead be ongoing relationships where I know that my decision today will affect the likelihood that the other player will cooperate in future. In a two-player game this gives a strong incentive to cooperate, but sadly this incentive becomes much weaker when the game involves larger numbers of players, since it then becomes more plausible that I can cheat whilst others continue to cooperate.

Game theory is a complex and developing field, but the prisoner's dilemma gives us a very powerful insight into some behaviour that we see in everyday life. You are likely to come across many other examples.[6] Some antisocial behaviour comes about when people do not consider the consequences of their actions, but the prisoner's dilemma shows that antisocial behaviour can sometimes be an entirely rational choice. The tragedy is that even if we know that everyone would be better off if we cooperated, the incentive to cheat can leave us all worse off. We should expect cheating as long as (i) the participants are selfish; (ii) they assume that their own choice has no effect on whether other people continue to cooperate. In these situations we might wish to look at ways to change incentives so as to deter cheating.

Box 4.3 Why are cartels unstable?

In Chapter 3 we saw that firms have an incentive to cooperate with each other rather than compete, since they will each make greater profits if they agree to restrict their output and keep prices high. However, there are two reasons why such cartels may not last. The first is that these agreements are generally illegal, so they only tend to last as long as they remain undiscovered. The second is the prisoner's dilemma, since each individual firm has an incentive to increase its market share by cheating: secretly undercutting its rivals by offering clients prices that are slightly below the level agreed inside the cartel. However, every firm has the same incentives and if all cheat then the cartel will collapse and prices and output will return to their competitive levels.

Cooperation is good for the members of the cartel, but bad for consumers. In this case consumers can be glad that the prisoner's dilemma sometimes undermines cartel agreements.

The most famous cartel is the Organization of the Petroleum Exporting Countries (**OPEC**). Its members are sovereign states which do not need to fear being accused of acting illegally, so unlike most cartels OPEC operates entirely in the open, aiming to keep global oil prices high by agreeing quotas which limit how much oil each member state produces. There appears to be a certain amount of cheating by smaller members, who anticipate that as long as they only exceed their quotas by a modest amount then the larger members (notably Saudi Arabia) are likely to tolerate this cheating rather than retaliate by increasing their own output and sending prices falling.

Summary

In this chapter we identified a number of market failures which are likely to lead to undesirable outcomes, even if people behave entirely rationally: (i) natural monopolies abusing their power; (ii) consumers lacking the information required to make sensible decisions; (iii) decisions which ignore the externalities imposed on other people; (iv) public goods. Even governments which believe strongly in the free market tend to intervene to correct such market failures.

The prisoner's dilemma helps explain why people may behave uncooperatively even if they are aware that they would all be better off if they cooperated. We return to the problems caused by the prisoner's dilemma in Chapter 11.

In Chapter 5 we consider psychological effects which may also lead to systematically bad decision-making, and where the government may wish to intervene to 'nudge' individuals to make better decisions. We also consider the labour and financial markets, where information and incentive problems are particularly severe.

CHAPTER 5
LABOUR MARKETS, FINANCE, AND BEHAVIOURAL ECONOMICS

We have come a long way already. We started by explaining how market economies can work—and often work fairly well—without a central plan, but in Chapter 4 we investigated some areas where markets do not work well, and how governments can respond. We continue with this theme in this chapter—our last on microeconomics—by considering labour markets and the financial sector. These are important parts of the economy but, as we shall see, they suffer from substantial information and incentive problems. We end by considering **behavioural economics** which uses insights from psychology to explore the ways in which consumer behaviour is often less rational than we assumed in Chapters 2 and 3.

Labour Markets

In the markets we have covered so far, demand has generally come from individuals and supply has come from firms. In labour markets the roles are reversed as individuals sell their services to firms in return for cash.

Despite this role reversal, we can regard the market for a particular type of labour (e.g. plumbers) as fairly similar to other markets. The supply curve is determined by the number of qualified individuals who are willing to work. This curve is likely to slope upwards, since a higher wage (the 'price' in this market) will encourage existing plumbers to work longer hours or to postpone their retirements, and in the long term it may encourage more people to obtain the skills required to work in this field.

The demand curve represents the number of workers that employers wish to hire at any given wage. Demand for accountants is likely to be inelastic because firms are legally required to have their accounts audited. Demand for other types of labour might be more elastic. Higher wages may lead firms to invest in automated technology to replace factory workers, and individuals might delay non-urgent plumbing projects.

The underlying forces driving these labour markets are similar to the markets we saw in earlier chapters. However, labour markets are badly affected by information problems. Hiring an incompetent plumber or a dishonest accountant can cause massive problems. Potential employers grasp at any available information in order to try to hire good staff. Appropriate qualifications and references from previous employers are an obvious starting point. Interviews are also widely used, but they may not be a very good indicator of the applicant's skills. Interviews may even make the situation worse if employees are hired because they are considered likeable, rather than necessarily being good at their jobs.

Educational establishments and professional bodies help combat this lack of information. Most obviously, they improve the skills of their students and award qualifications designed to give a fairly objective indication of the level of skill achieved. They can also play a more subtle role. For example, suppose that you were offered a place at an elite university to study a subject that you considered utterly irrelevant to your career. This degree could nevertheless be a useful signal to future employers that you were talented enough to be offered a place at this prestigious institution. This could be very valuable even if you don't actually learn anything useful!

Problems with Incentives

Labour markets suffer information problems just like many other markets, but they also have some unique problems of their own. You might have to worry about buying a poor-quality car, but you don't need to worry that it might become demotivated or decide to work for someone else instead.

When we buy an item in a shop we want to pay the lowest possible price. The same might not be true in labour markets, because these involve an ongoing relationship between employer and employee. If the employer pays the bare minimum needed to attract suitable employees then these employees know that they could easily get an equally good job elsewhere. This is likely to lead to high employee turnover. It also means that employees have little incentive to care about keeping their employer happy, since the threat of losing their job holds little sting.

Instead, it may make perfect sense for employers to pay more than the market-clearing wage: this gives each employee a strong incentive to hold onto this job rather than look for another. Such **efficiency wages** imply that the market will not settle to the supply=demand equilibrium we would expect in other markets. Instead there will be an excess supply of people who would like to get a job at this high wage, but are unable to (Figure 5.1). Employees already earning this wage will be motivated to do a good job out of fear that losing it will leave them having to take a lower-paid job elsewhere. Note that here we are considering supply and demand for specific types of labour, such as plumbers and accountants, but macroeconomic effects mean that it would be a mistake to assume that total unemployment in the economy is simply due to high wages—we see why in Chapter 8.

Efficiency wages also help prevent adverse selection. Just like our used car example in Chapter 4, individuals who are selling their labour are likely to have much better information about their own skills and motivation than their potential employers. This

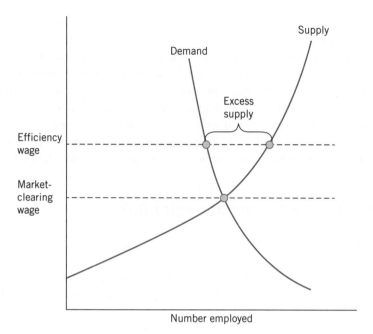

Figure 5.1 Efficiency wage

means that offering a job at a modest wage might mean that the only workers willing to accept this offer are those who know that they are worse than average!

Another problem is that employers generally cannot observe everything that their employees do. Instead they have to trust their employees to do a good job even when not being watched. Unfortunately employees may have their own rather different goals, such as preferring to be lazy if they think they can get away with it. Similarly, the managers of large companies are expected to work on behalf of their shareholders, but they may have different motives: increasing the perks of the job (such as a company jet); preferring a quiet life rather than addressing the difficult decisions that are needed to keep the firm profitable; or boosting their own status by increasing the firm's size (e.g. by taking over other firms) regardless of whether this is profitable.[1] This problem can affect any relationship which involves delegation. For example, it explains the use of 'nanny cams' which allow nervous parents to observe how their nannies treat their children when they think they are not being watched.

The employer–employee relationship may also need to be flexible in order to adjust to changing circumstances. For example, promotion is used to reflect an employee's increasing skill and experience. There are many situations in which people are willing to take a relatively poorly paid job on the understanding that there will subsequently be opportunities for promotion and pay rises. Such issues are likely to be discussed by employer and employee, but they are seldom written down and are known instead as the **implicit contract**. For some jobs this can be more important than what is explicit in the formal contract that is signed. A belief that this implicit contract has not been honoured can be a key factor leading employees to become disillusioned and seek better jobs elsewhere.

There is often a high degree of government intervention in labour markets, for example in the form of minimum wages or health and safety legislation. **Trade unions** are also significant in some industries. Their role can best be thought of as similar to the cartels we saw in Chapter 3, aiming to increase wages for their members.

In summary, the markets for specific types of labour are driven by supply and demand, just like other markets. However, information and incentive problems help explain some of the unique features of the labour market that we often take for granted.

What Does the Financial Sector Do?

The financial sector forms a significant part of the economy, including the banks that we see on our high streets and the global financial institutions found in major financial centres. Some of these institutions provide specific services (such as insurance), but most are involved in borrowing and lending. We can regard this as a market which exchanges *cash now* for *cash later*.

Cash now is exchanged for a slightly larger amount of cash later—how much larger depends on the **interest rate** charged, which is the price of funds borrowed in this market. A high interest rate encourages lending (the supply of cash now), whilst a low interest rate encourages borrowing (demand). However, as we shall see in Chapters 8–9, this is not an entirely free market price, since central banks set the level of key interest rates as an important part of macroeconomic policy.

Borrowing and lending is not confined to some capitalist elite—it is something that we are all likely to find beneficial at some stage. Whilst working, we should be saving for our pensions: supplying cash now in exchange for cash later. At other times we might be borrowing (demanding cash now): perhaps a student loan to support us during higher education or a mortgage to buy a flat. It is not just individuals who need to borrow. Growing companies need to borrow in order to buy bigger premises and extra equipment, and governments borrow to finance expenditure in excess of their tax revenue.

Financial institutions play an important quality control function in this market. Ideally, we would like funds to be lent to innovative companies with strong growth prospects (the next Apple or Dyson) whilst banks reject borrowers who are fraudulent or over-optimistic. Unfortunately, distinguishing between good and bad borrowers can be difficult. Perfect foresight cannot be expected, but getting these decisions right as often as possible can have a big impact on the dynamism and growth of the economy. However, the system failed spectacularly in the run-up to the 2008 financial crisis.

Changing circumstances might mean that a person or institution who has previously lent money suddenly needs that money back. Debt contracts generally do not allow lenders to demand early repayment, but there is a neat solution: the lender simply sells the debt contract to someone else. The original lender obtains the cash they need, whilst future repayments of the loan go to the new owner of the contract. Such a tradable debt contract is known as a **bond**. Shares (also known as **equities**) are technically not debt, since they make the holder a part owner of the company involved, but they have a very similar function: firms issue shares in order to raise the cash they need to expand, whilst investors who buy these shares can exchange them for cash when needed, by selling their shares to another investor on the **stock exchange**.

Prices of shares and bonds vary in response to economic news which is perceived to affect the future profitability of companies or the likelihood that borrowers might default on their loans. These price movements are reported in the financial press every day. However, as we shall see shortly, individuals are less rational than they might admit, so emotional and psychological factors ('market sentiment') also play an important part.

What Caused the 2008 Global Financial Crisis?

Much has been written about the causes of the crisis, but a key factor was information problems similar to those we saw in Chapter 4.

As we have seen, information problems come about when buyers cannot properly observe the quality of what they are purchasing. A key problem in finance is determining the level of risk. Specifically, can we rely on borrowers to repay their loans? This has always been a difficult problem, but it became even harder in the years running up to the crisis since:

1. Loans were being transformed into increasingly complex tradable assets (with names such as MBS, CDO, ABS, etc.). These had some appealing characteristics, but they made it harder to keep track of the underlying borrowers' ability to pay.

2. Many investors relied on specialist Credit Rating Agencies to figure out how risky these assets were. But the ratings given were far too optimistic, partly because these agencies were paid by the issuers of the assets, so they had an incentive to give high ratings in order to keep their clients happy.

As a result, most people involved were pretty relaxed about the fact that US housing loans were being made to more risky 'sub-prime' borrowers. The people responsible for making these loans had an incentive to make as many as possible. They had little incentive to worry about who they lent to as long as someone else was willing to buy these loans from them, and good credit ratings meant that there generally were buyers. Some of these loans involved outright fraud which exaggerated the borrower's ability to repay. Increasing numbers of borrowers subsequently started to default and institutions found that some loans they had thought were safe were in fact almost worthless. Large financial institutions suddenly faced the prospect of going bust.

Such information problems are by no means unique to the financial sector. Indeed, loans can be regarded as pretty similar to used cars, since in both markets it can be hard to tell which ones are useless. As default rates in the US housing market rose, it became obvious that some lenders must have lost a lot of money. Everyone was nervous of lending to institutions which might turn out to have already lost huge amounts in bad housing loans (implying that these institutions might, in turn, be unable to repay what they themselves had borrowed). But these housing loans had been transformed into other forms and then sold on to other institutions—often changing hands many times—so it was very difficult to tell which institutions were the losers. In this situation the rational response was to assume the worst and stop lending to anyone. This triggered a general **credit crunch** as even institutions which were not actually at risk suddenly found that no one was willing to lend to them.

This problem was transformed into a truly global crisis because financial institutions are interconnected to a much greater extent than in other sectors, giving rise to **systemic risk**. If one supermarket suddenly goes out of business this is likely to be good news for other supermarkets, which increase their market share. Not so in finance. The collapse of one bank dramatically increases the risk that other banks will fail, since (i) banks often lend to each other; and (ii) the collapse of one bank may result in nervous savers withdrawing their deposits from other banks.

Information problems and systemic risk gave rise to a wave of collapses among financial institutions that had been thought to be perfectly safe. Governments concluded that they could not risk letting this vicious circle get any worse, so they felt compelled to bail out collapsed institutions with huge amounts of public funds.

The terrible costs of this crisis and the subsequent global recession have led to many proposals for reform. Regulators have already tightened rules on bonuses: paying a large proportion of employees' pay in this form motivates them to make profits for their employers, but it also encourages them to take high levels of risk. There have also been attempts to reduce information problems by making it easier to observe the risks that each financial institution is taking. Small financial institutions can take large risks if they choose, but only if the government can afford to let them go bust without triggering major systemic risks. By contrast, reformers are agreed that institutions that are too big to be allowed to fail must be made more 'boring' and prevented from taking such high levels of risk again.[2]

Behavioural Economics

In Chapters 2 and 3 we assumed that consumers make rational choices which maximize their utility. However, over recent years research into behavioural economics has shown that our decisions are not always as rational as we might like to think.

Modern life throws many complex problems at us, but we are not always able to give them the clear and dispassionate consideration that they require. Daniel Kahneman, a pioneer in behavioural economics, identified two very different types of decision-making: 'System 1' is quick, emotional and instinctive, whilst 'System 2' is slower, more dispassionate and logical.[3] The latter is closer to the careful utility-maximizing behaviour that we assumed in earlier chapters. System 1 behaviour can be very different.

For example, we tend to assess something new or unknown by making a snap judgement based on whether it reminds us of a previous experience. This is quick, and may be appropriate in some circumstances, but it often biases our judgement by giving too much weight to the experiences that are most vivid and easily remembered. This can make us particularly bad at judging probabilities. Our decisions may also depend on the exact **framing** of the choices. For example, you may well reject an investment which could lose half its value, but your response might be very different if instead I told you that even in the worst case the investment would keep half of its value. Logically these are identical, but a different presentation can trigger very different emotional reactions which influence our choices.

However, we should not be too critical of ourselves. Thinking is slow and hard work, and using quick-and-dirty rules of thumb might be perfectly sensible if the time and effort saved more than outweigh the consequences of a few avoidable errors. Our instincts evolved to help our ancestors survive in a dangerous and violent world. Mistakenly jumping at shadows was a small price to pay if their instincts also helped them respond quickly to real threats. We should not be too surprised if the instincts that kept our ancestors alive are less well suited to modern needs such as filling in a tax return or choosing a pension plan.

The evolutionary need for rapid decisions can explain some of our behavioural quirks. Others appear to reflect an emotional need to feel good about ourselves. Are you a better than average driver? If so, you are in good company: surveys show around 80 per cent of us believe that we are better than average.[4] We are also overconfident when we make estimates or forecasts, dramatically underestimating the probability that we will turn out to be badly wrong. Similar biases affect our ability to learn, since changing our minds involves a painful admission that we were wrong. Instead, when presented with new information we tend to focus on the parts which confirm our existing views and downplay the rest (confirmation bias).[5] Even when our forecasts turn out to be wrong, we tend to reinvent them afterwards, convincing ourselves that 'we knew it all along' (hindsight bias).

Our desire to flatter ourselves also affects how we interpret events. We tend to regard good outcomes as having been due to our own actions, whilst we dismiss bad outcomes as 'outside our control' or 'acts of God' (attribution bias). Finally, studies have repeatedly shown that our judgement is strongly affected by the opinions of those around us. We are social animals. Standing out from the crowd tends to make us uncomfortable, so we find it much easier to agree with the **groupthink**.

Our financial decisions in particular can be badly affected by these behavioural biases. The image of our financial institutions as dominated by overconfident men who are unable to admit their mistakes has become a stereotype, but it is one that many will recognize.[6] The late 1990s dot-com boom saw groupthink (everyone agreed that shares in new technology companies were worth vast amounts) and overconfidence which neglected the possibility of a crash. Similar complacency appears to have preceded the crisis of 2008.

Most of these biases are entirely subconscious. Greater awareness of our flaws might sometimes help us avoid mistakes. For example, noticing when we are making a snap System 1 decision may allow us to replace it with a more deliberate System 2 decision. Institutions could be designed to include safeguards against emotionally driven biases that lead to poor decision-making. Governments around the world have also started

using behavioural insights to help 'nudge' our behaviour, for example by framing decisions in ways which encourage us to make choices that are likely to be in our long-term
interests.[7] Some might distrust such government action to alter our decision-making,
but at least it is designed (however imperfectly) to improve our own welfare and the welfare of those around us. By contrast, advertising and marketing campaigns use similar
psychological insights on a vastly greater scale to encourage us to buy products that we
would not otherwise have chosen.

Behavioural economics is an exciting and fast-developing field which can offer richer
and more complex descriptions of our decision-making. It shows that we often act less
like the cool and rational intellectuals that we would like to think, and rather more
like the scared, lazy, and insecure apes that in evolutionary terms we still are. However,
this does not invalidate Chapters 2 and 3. The assumption that consumers coldly and
rationally maximize their utility is clearly simplistic, but it successfully explains a lot of
the behaviour that we see day-to-day. This model is an oversimplification, but a very
useful one—for example, it is likely to be perfectly adequate in explaining how demand
reacts following a price cut. More complex situations are likely to require more complex
models which take account of behavioural effects.

Box 5.1 Sunk costs—letting bygones be bygones

Suppose that the government has spent £30bn building a nuclear power station, but
during construction the price of uranium has soared and wholesale electricity prices
have fallen. As a result the latest projections suggest that the plant will never recoup its
construction costs, and will make an additional operating loss of around £1bn per year.
What should the government do?

It would be very tempting to operate the plant anyway. Leaving it unused feels like an
obscene waste of £30bn, but this would be the best option. To see this, we have to accept
that the £30bn has already been wasted and cannot now be recovered: it is a **sunk cost**.

We would much prefer not to have built the plant, but that option is long gone. In other
circumstances sale or conversion to another use might be possible, but this is unlikely to be
practical for such specialized equipment which is now loss-making in its designed role. The
only choices we now have are: (a) leave the plant unused and accept that we have wasted
£30bn; (b) operate the plant as planned, wasting £30bn plus an additional £1bn operating
loss each year. The better option in this scenario is clearly to leave the plant unused.[8]

This decision is difficult partly because of the emotions involved. Our **regret** over the decision to build the plant is likely to be extremely powerful. It also takes humility to admit
(even to ourselves) that a mistake was made and that it is better not to waste even more
money by operating the plant. Unfortunately, decisions of this type are typically made by
politicians or senior corporate managers—people not known for their humility—so it
should come as no surprise if they sometimes press on rather than admit their mistake.

Summary

Information problems are particularly severe in the financial sector and in labour markets. This helps explain some of the features of these markets that we often take for granted.

More generally, incentives matter. They are key to attracting the right employees and motivating for them. Inappropriate incentives also encouraged excessively risky behaviour in the financial sector.

Behavioural economics is an exciting and growing field which offers insights into why our behaviour can sometimes be very different from the rational utility maximization that we assumed in earlier chapters.

CHAPTER 6
MICROECONOMICS SUMMARY

We started this book with the astonishing observation that market economies generally work fairly well without any central plan. As we explored how markets operate, this observation became less surprising than it first seemed. Suppliers naturally adjust their prices and the quantities they produce when they see excess supply or excess demand. Correspondingly, consumers adjust their demand as prices shift. These reactions are pretty obvious—participants certainly don't need to have studied economics in order to react appropriately. Nevertheless, this process achieves something that centrally planned economies found very difficult: supplying goods for which there is demand without generating persistent gluts or shortages.

But markets are far from perfect. We identified market failures where even if people behave entirely rationally we should expect markets to generate undesirable outcomes. Government intervention might help in these situations (natural monopolies, information failures, externalities, and public goods). Inappropriate government intervention risks making things worse rather than better (government failure), but in practice there are no pure free market economies. Even in the USA, where the idea of small government has long been widely supported, the government intervenes substantially in the economy and government expenditure accounts for 35 per cent of US GDP.[1]

A common criticism of economics is that it makes assumptions that are clearly unrealistic, but this criticism misunderstands why we make such assumptions. In these chapters we have used a variety of different models. Our initial model of consumer behaviour was very simple: it assumed that people make themselves as happy as possible by buying things. We do not really believe that people care only about their consumption, but we made this assumption because in many situations this very simple model is useful, since it predicts fairly accurately how consumers will respond to changes in prices or incomes or the range of goods that is available. In other situations we might expect this model to be inaccurate, so we would turn to more complex alternatives which might include strategic behaviour (Chapter 4) or behavioural effects (Chapter 5).

Such simplifying assumptions are by no means unique to economics. Physicists know that relativistic and quantum effects mean that Newton's laws of motion are only approximations. But for everyday purposes they are perfectly adequate approximations, so engineers continue to use them without producing machines that don't function or buildings that fall down. It is a matter of choosing an appropriate analytic tool for the job at hand.

It is also important to realize that simple economic models are intended as descriptions, not prescriptions. Regarding consumers as selfish and coldly rational utility-maximizers is an adequately accurate description of their behaviour in many situations. It is not a recommendation that people should behave in this way! People are driven by emotional needs. They can be incredibly loving and charitable, and the world is a much better place as a result. We will return in Chapter 11 to consider the wider factors that tend to make people happy.

The first half of this book aimed to provide a range of insights which can be used for business purposes (such as elasticities, monopoly, and price discrimination), for policy purposes (how to respond to market failures), or simply to give us a better understanding of the behaviour we see in the world around us (the prisoner's dilemma, behavioural economics).

In the second half we shall turn to macroeconomics in order to explain problems such as inflation and unemployment, and identify policies that can be used to combat them. Once again, judgement is needed: we will find that the simplest model (assuming that the whole economy can be regarded as simply one big labour market) turns out to be extremely misleading. However, other models will allow us to analyse these problems, understand policy mistakes that have been made in the past, and identify challenges that remain for the future.

PART TWO
MACROECONOMICS

In the second part of this book we turn our attention to macroeconomic phenomena such as inflation and unemployment. These affect the economy as a whole, so we must take a 'big picture' view, in contrast to microeconomics where we considered the decisions made by individual firms and **households**.

As before, we aim to explain fundamental economic principles that apply to all economies. For illustrative purposes we generally use the UK as an example, but the principles involved apply much more widely.

We aim to get as quickly as possible to real policy issues. In particular, we will explain how the economy can get stuck in a recession and how fiscal and monetary policies can be used to try to boost it out (Chapter 8); the causes and cures for inflation (Chapter 9); international trade (Chapter 10) and long-term growth and welfare (Chapter 11). However, before we can do any of this we need to be a bit clearer about what economic activity is and how we can measure it. We address this in Chapter 7.

CHAPTER 7
MEASURING ECONOMIC ACTIVITY

Politicians and economic commentators talk a lot about **gross domestic product** (GDP). This can be defined as the total amount of goods and services that the economy produces each year. Figure 7.1 shows how UK GDP has grown since 1970. The dotted line shows what the UK actually did produce each year, whilst 'potential GDP' is an estimate of the level of output that the economy could sustain without leading to **inflation**.

At first sight Figure 7.1 makes us wonder what all the fuss is about, since ever-improving technology seems to mean that we are getting inexorably richer every year. However, those seemingly small fluctuations have a big impact. If actual GDP is below potential (a negative **GDP gap**), then the economy is producing less than it could and we are likely to see unemployment. Unemployment rose in each of the **recessions** shown in Figure 7.2: in the early 1980s, the early 1990s, and following the global financial crisis of 2008. Unemployment makes us poorer on average and brings misery to those who lose their jobs. It is important to explain why recessions occur, and hopefully also find some ways to reduce their severity. Conversely, a booming economy will reduce unemployment, but is likely to lead to inflation, which can also be extremely damaging. Macroeconomic policy aims for a 'Goldilocks' economy which is running neither too hot (inflation) nor too cold (recession).

Our first step in understanding why these fluctuations occur is to gain a better understanding of what GDP is and how it is measured. We could simply add up the total value of the goods and services produced by every firm in the country. For most firms this would just be the total value of everything they sell—in other words their total revenue. However, the answer this gave us would be too large, because of double counting. For example, we would have included the total revenue of the car industry and the steel industry, but the value of the steel used in making cars will already be reflected in the total revenue of car manufacturers, since the price they charge for cars must cover the cost of this steel, as well as all their other costs. To avoid this we need to make a distinction between **final goods and services** (things that we buy and consume, such as food and haircuts and cars) and **intermediates**, which are bought by firms and used to produce other things.

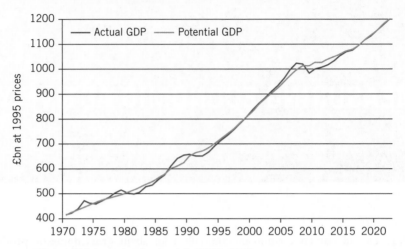

Figure 7.1 UK real GDP (actual and potential), 1970–2022
Source: International Monetary Fund (IMF forecasts 2017–22)

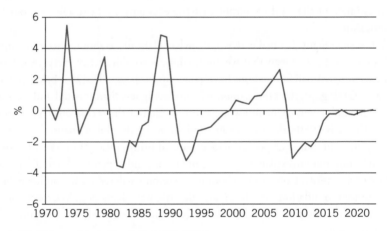

Figure 7.2 UK GDP gap (% of potential), 1970–2022
Source: International Monetary Fund (IMF forecasts 2017–22)

Figure 7.3 illustrates the problem of double counting. In this simple example cars are the only final good produced in the economy. The column on the left shows the total revenue of car manufacturers. Other firms produce intermediate goods: steel for use by the car manufacturers, and iron ore for use in the steel industry. Summing the total revenue of all three industries would give us £7bn. This includes the £4bn revenue of the car industry and the £2bn revenue of the steel industry, but the whole of this £2bn has already been included as the part of car manufacturers' revenue which they use to pay for this steel. Similarly, the £2bn revenue of the steel industry includes the £1bn that steel manufacturers pay for the iron ore they use, but we have also included this as the revenue of the mining industry.[1]

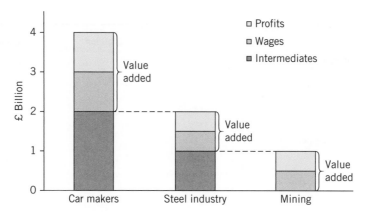

Figure 7.3 Avoiding double counting

One way around the problem of double counting is simply to ignore intermediate goods such as steel and iron ore, and measure GDP as total expenditure on final goods and services. After all, it is only these that contribute directly to consumer welfare. Intermediate goods are only important to the extent that they contribute to making these final goods and services. In our simple example, GDP is just the £4bn spent on cars.

This gives us our first method for calculating GDP: add up all the final goods and services produced by the UK economy. Thus GDP comprises: (i) consumer spending by UK households; (ii) consumption paid for by the UK Government (e.g. on providing health and education services and defence); (iii) **investment** spending by UK firms;[2] and (iv) UK exports to the rest of the world (conversely we need to subtract imports, since these are not produced in the UK). The first section of Table 7.1 shows GDP measured by this method. The majority of expenditure comes from household consumption (65 per cent), but government and investment spending are also important. Summing all these components gives us total UK GDP of £1,870 billion.

We could instead consider the **value added** by each industry. For example, the car industry is useful because it turns raw materials into cars. In Figure 7.3 the value added by car manufacturers is £2bn, which is the difference between the £4bn value of the cars they produced and the £2bn of the intermediates they used. Similarly, steel manufacturers convert £1bn of raw materials into £2bn of steel (£1bn value added). In our simple example the mining industry does not use any intermediate goods, so the whole of its £1bn revenue is value added.[3] Thus, instead of summing the revenue of every firm in the economy, we can avoid the double counting problem by just summing the value added by each firm. When we do this we find total value added of £4bn (the same as total expenditure on final goods, which is simply the £4bn spent on cars). This is our second method for measuring GDP.

The second section of Table 7.1 shows the value added by each sector of the UK economy. This gives us important insights into the structure of the economy. For example,

Table 7.1 UK GDP by three different methods (2015)

		£ billion	% of GDP
Expenditure category			
Household consumption		1217	65.1
Government consumption		362	19.4
Investment		328	17.5
Trade balance (=exports–imports)		–39	–2.1
	GDP	1870	100.0
Industrial sector			
Agriculture		10	0.5
Manufacturing		165	9.0
Electricity, gas, water, mining		58	3.0
Construction		98	5.2
Distribution, hotels, and restaurants		307	16.4
Information and communications		104	5.6
Finance and insurance		122	6.5
Professional, support, and other services		470	25.1
Education, health, public administration, and defence		309	16.5
Taxes on products less subsidies		227	12.1
	GDP	1870	100.0
Gross incomes			
Profits		589	31.5
Wages and salaries (inc. self-employed)		1054	56.4
Taxes on products less subsidies		227	12.1
	GDP	1870	100.0

Source: Adapted from Office for National Statistics data licensed under the Open Government Licence v.3.0

we can see that manufacturing now only accounts for only 9 per cent of UK GDP. This is a spectacular change. For more than 100 years following the Industrial Revolution, the UK economy was dominated by manufacturing but, like other **developed economies**, over the past century it has instead become a 'knowledge economy' focused on producing services. Summing the value added by each sector gives us the same figure as before for total UK GDP: £1,870bn.[4]

Our final method of measuring GDP is as total income. Consider what happens to the revenue generated by firms. Most firms use some of their revenue to pay for the intermediate goods and services that they use. They use a significant proportion of the

Box 7.1 Estimating GDP

GDP is the cash value of all the final goods and services produced in the UK economy. This rises either if the economy produces more goods and services, or if prices rise (inflation). It is important to distinguish between these two effects. Increased production raises average material standards of living. By contrast, inflation does nothing to improve living standards and may well be a source of economic instability—we discuss this in Chapter 9.

To separate these two effects, GDP must first be estimated in cash terms using any of the three methods discussed above. This is known as **nominal GDP**. We can easily calculate how much this has risen since our last estimate. To work out how much of this rise was due to inflation, the average price level (covering all the main final goods and services produced in the economy) is recorded at the start and end of this period. If nominal GDP increased by 3 per cent and inflation was 2 per cent then our economy must have produced 1 per cent more goods and services. In order to distinguish it from the effect of inflation we refer to this as 1 per cent growth in **real GDP**.

Nominal UK GDP rose by an average of 8 per cent per annum between 1970 and 2016, but this was mainly due to inflation. Real GDP growth averaged only 2.1 per cent per annum, but even this was sufficient to see real GDP almost treble over the period shown in Figure 7.1, representing a very welcome increase in average living standards.

Estimating GDP raises other statistical difficulties. It is relatively easy to measure output when goods are sold, but it is harder to measure the value of the services provided by workers who do not charge for their services, such as NHS doctors, police, and other civil servants. In **developing countries** subsistence farmers (who consume their own produce) tend not to show up in GDP, unlike very similar farmers who sell their output. Similarly, unpaid child care and volunteer work are not recorded, but similar services are recorded if they are paid for. In some countries the size of unrecorded **black market** transactions is also an important issue. Government statisticians do their best, but we need to recognize the potential flaws in the GDP figures in order to ensure that we are making like-for-like comparisons.[5]

remainder to pay their employees' wages. Anything left after this is (gross) profit. Thus the value added by a firm is simply composed of profits and wages. The same is true of every firm, so instead of summing the value added by each one, we could simply sum the wages earned by every employee and the total profits earned by the owners of these firms. This method of calculating GDP is shown in the third section of Table 7.1.

Our three different methods for calculating GDP give us identical answers, since they each include the same underlying components, just summed in a different order. Figure 7.3 illustrates this: the £4bn expenditure on final goods (cars) represents total value added in the different sectors of the economy and this in turn is simply the wages and profits generated in each sector.

Exploring how GDP is measured has told us something about the economy which was not immediately apparent, and which turns out to be very important: that total expenditure on final goods = total value added in all the different sectors of the economy = total incomes (wages plus profits).

Summary

GDP per person is a useful measure of average material living standards, but it would be a mistake to regard it as a measure of national happiness. We return to this point in Chapter 11. Nevertheless, for all its flaws, fluctuations in GDP tell us something important about the economy, and it is very beneficial if we can learn how to reduce the size of such booms and recessions.

We have spent time exploring how GDP is measured because this leads us to a conclusion that was not immediately obvious: that every pound spent on final goods and services in the economy ultimately ends up being someone's income (either as wages or as profits). This turns out to be a vital insight when we turn to explaining economic booms and recessions in Chapter 8.

CHAPTER 8
EXPLAINING UNEMPLOYMENT

Unemployment rose steadily in the Great Depression of the early 1930s, peaking at an unprecedented 17 per cent. Traditional models of the economy could not explain this. The conventional view at the time was that the entire labour market was just like the market for eggs in Chapter 2. One group has something to sell (individuals selling their labour) whilst the other (employers) needs labour and is willing to pay cash. As shown in Figure 8.1, the total amount of labour employed in the economy was assumed to be determined by the demand curve for labour (the total number of people that firms wish to employ) and the corresponding supply curve. The price of this labour is simply the wage per employee.[1]

Unemployment by definition means that the supply of labour is greater than demand, leaving excess supply (individuals who would like to work but cannot find a job). This was assumed to be because the price of labour was too high. High wages increase the supply of labour, for example by encouraging existing employees to work longer hours or to remain in employment when they might otherwise have considered retiring. Conversely, demand for labour is reduced as employers react to high wages by seeking to reduce their number of employees, for example by investing in labour-saving machinery or simply cutting production.

Given this view of the labour market, the cure for unemployment seemed obvious: wages must fall. Indeed, the existence of an excess supply of labour should itself put downward pressure on wages, pushing the economy back to the market equilibrium where supply equals demand. Wages did indeed fall during the early 1930s—the mystery was that unemployment kept rising. John Maynard Keynes solved this mystery, and in doing so he changed the way people think about macroeconomics in much the same way that Einstein changed the way that people think about physics.

To understand this we need to return to the assumptions that we explored in Chapter 2 when we saw how a demand curve is derived. We know that a lot of factors other than the price of the product can affect demand, such as consumer incomes and tastes and the prices of substitutes. If the price of eggs changes but none of these other factors do, then we move from one point on the demand curve to another. If, instead, one of these other factors changes, then we have a demand shock which shifts the whole demand curve. This was a useful distinction to make in the market for eggs, but it turns out to be very misleading when we consider the overall labour market for the whole economy.

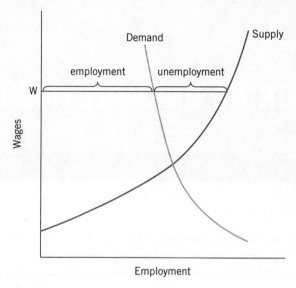

Figure 8.1 The classical view of unemployment

Suppose that wages do indeed fall whilst nothing else changes. We saw in Chapter 7 that wages are the main component of household incomes, so when wages fall, household incomes must also fall. This in turn means that households are likely to cut their expenditure on goods and services. When they do, firms will find that they are selling less than before and will cut back on production. This implies a leftward shift in the demand for labour, since at any given wage firms now desire fewer employees than they did before (Figure 8.2).

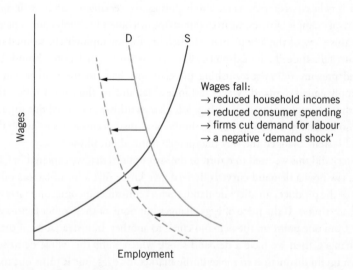

Figure 8.2 'Demand shock' caused by falling wages

In the market for eggs we could sensibly talk about a shift from one point on the demand curve to another as the price of eggs changes, whilst all other relevant factors remain unchanged. We cannot do this for the aggregate labour market, since the other factors will never remain unchanged: a shift in average wages in the economy will itself cause a leftward shift in demand for labour (a negative demand shock) as firms find that demand for their products has fallen, and so reduce their demand for labour.

In the egg market we would expect any excess supply to be temporary, since it will lead to a reduced price which shifts the market towards the point where supply equals demand. But Keynes realized that in the labour market a reduction in wages can make the situation worse rather than better because it shifts the labour demand curve.[2] Indeed this is exactly what was seen in the 1930s: wages fell, but unemployment increased as firms reacted to the fall in demand for their products.

The traditional (**classical economics**) view of the labour market was reassuring, since it suggested that high levels of unemployment would only ever be temporary. The Keynesian view suggests instead that the main force driving the aggregate labour market is the feedback from consumer spending onto firms' demand for labour. This means that we can imagine the economy in one of two states. In good times we might see high aggregate consumer spending leading to high levels of demand for goods and hence high employment. This is the virtuous circle shown in Figure 8.3. The economy might instead settle into the vicious circle where low consumer spending leads to low demand for goods and low employment and thus low household incomes, cementing the lower consumer spending in place.

The classical view assumed that, like other markets, there was a single equilibrium for the labour market with supply=demand, implying zero unemployment. The Keynesian view suggests instead that there may be more than one equilibrium, and that a catalytic event might push the economy from one to another. Indeed this is a fairly realistic picture of recent history. Up until 2007 most developed economies were in the high spending/high employment virtuous circle, but the financial crisis of 2008 saw nervous consumers and investors cut their spending, pushing these economies into a low spending/low employment equilibrium.[3] Many economies endured years of high unemployment as they struggled to escape from this vicious circle.

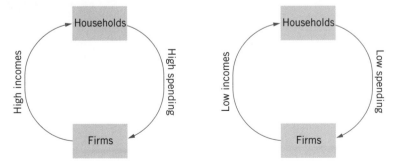

Figure 8.3 Virtuous and vicious circles

Withdrawals and Injections

The Keynesian model allows us to explain persistent unemployment, whereas the classical view could not. However, Figure 8.3 is too simplistic since not all household income is spent on goods and services. Some is paid to the government as taxes, and households are likely to save some of the remainder (Figure 8.4). The flow of household income into taxes tends to reduce the amount that is spent on things produced by UK firms, and thus threatens to push the economy into the low spending/low employment loop. But that is not the whole picture, since the government also spends money on services such as health, education, and defence. Similarly the flow of income that is saved by households (rather than being spent) is offset by the fact that firms borrow money in order to finance investment spending. Saving and taxes represent **withdrawals** of expenditure from the economy, whilst investment and government spending represent offsetting **injections** of additional spending which tend to boost demand and increase employment.

These withdrawals and injections give us two policies which can be used to try to jump-start the economy out of recession:

1. A change in interest rates can alter the balance between saving and investment. Cutting interest rates will tend to increase investment and consumption (since firms and households can borrow more cheaply) and discourage saving (savers are offered less attractive returns). This increases an injection of spending into the economy (investment) and reduces the corresponding withdrawal (saving). This is the basis

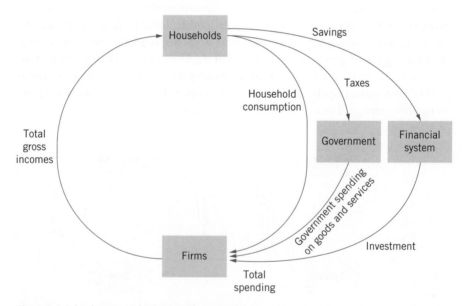

Figure 8.4 Injections and withdrawals of expenditure

for **monetary policy**, and it is precisely for this reason that the Bank of England cut interest rates from 5.75 per cent in early 2007 to only 0.5 per cent after the financial crisis as collapsing business and consumer confidence threatened to push the economy into a deep depression.[4]

2. The government can also increase its own expenditure (an injection of spending) or reduce taxation (which tends to increase consumer expenditure). This is **fiscal policy**. If existing sources of expenditure (consumer spending, investment, and government spending on goods and services) are too low, then the economy may be stuck in the low expenditure/low employment vicious circle. Extra government spending or tax cuts may be enough to shift the economy into the higher expenditure/high employment loop.[5]

We can now explain why the economy sometimes suffers recessions, and how the government can try to prevent such recessions using fiscal policy (higher government spending/lower taxes) or monetary policy (lower interest rates). However, these policies cannot be expected to remove GDP fluctuations entirely, since the vicious and virtuous circles discussed above tend to exacerbate the effect of unexpected shifts in demand. For example, a global recession could reduce demand for UK exports by £1bn, but this will in turn reduce total incomes in the UK and thus reduce expenditure by UK consumers as well. These secondary effects could lead to a total reduction in UK GDP that is several times larger than the initial £1bn reduction in export demand. This is known as the **multiplier**.

The bad news is that the multiplier means that even small shocks can have a substantial impact, making the economy unstable. The good news is that the multiplier also magnifies the impact of changes in fiscal and monetary policy, making them more powerful tools for stabilizing GDP. The multiplier additionally means that there is likely to be a significant lag before the full effects of these policies become apparent. This makes it hard to fine-tune the economy, since fiscal and monetary policy adjustments must be based on forecasts of the economy at least a year or two ahead. Setting policy has often been compared to driving whilst only looking in the rear-view mirror. The results can only be as good as the economic forecasts that are used, and policymakers will inevitably have to react after the event to unexpected shocks such as the 2008 crisis.

Summary

We have seen that applying microeconomic principles to the whole economy can be very misleading. Classical economics argued that the labour market is just like the market for eggs, so unemployment should only ever be temporary, since it will disappear as wages fall.

However, as we saw in Chapter 7, every piece of expenditure on final goods and services ultimately becomes someone's income. This explains how the economy can get stuck in a vicious circle of low employment and low expenditure. It also shows how fiscal and monetary policies can be used to try to boost the economy out of such a recession.

Nevertheless, our picture of the economy is still very simple. In Chapter 9 we extend it in order to explain inflation, and in Chapter 10 we consider exports and imports.

CHAPTER 9
INFLATION

In Chapter 2 we looked at what happens to demand when the price of one good rises whilst the prices of other goods stay unchanged. For example, we considered a rise in coffee prices following a bad harvest. This price rise could be regarded as a useful signal to consumers that coffee had become scarcer and that they might wish to switch to alternatives.

General inflation plays no such useful role. Instead it represents a situation in which all prices tend to rise. This is usually measured by changes in an index such as the CPI (**Consumer Price Index**), which is the average price of the goods and services consumed by the average household.[1] Figure 9.1 shows the annual percentage increase in this index. Inflation remained fairly low in the 1950s and 1960s, then jumped spectacularly in the 1970s and only slowly settled back to its previous levels.

Before we go further it is worth asking whether inflation is really a problem. Unemployment is associated with reduced GDP and hence lower average living standards, and it is a source of misery for those who lose their jobs. By contrast, prices are just a way of measuring the relative value of different goods and services. As long as our wages increase in line with prices, does inflation really matter?

The huge pile of banknotes in Figure 9.2 provides one answer to this question. Despite appearances, this woman has not won the lottery. She is burning the cash in the stove. The picture is from Germany in the 1920s after **hyperinflation** had left banknotes completely worthless. During just four months of 1923 wholesale prices rose by a factor of ten million.

But does the value of cash really matter? It does, because not all prices rise by the same amount. Those who hold assets which do not rise (such as banknotes or most government bonds) face financial ruin as these assets become worthless. If prices are rising significantly every day, then the overwhelming priority when you collect your pay is to spend it immediately rather than be left holding cash which is losing value every day. In this situation long-term planning and investment are abandoned. More generally, if inflation is high it also tends to be volatile, greatly increasing uncertainty about the future. A low and stable level of inflation is the only way to avoid this. Even the 15–25 per cent annual inflation seen in the UK in the 1970s could be enough to deter people

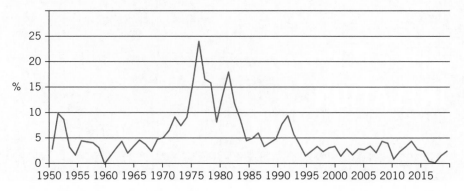

Figure 9.1 UK inflation (% per annum)
Source: Adapted from Office for National Statistics data licensed under the Open Government Licence v.3.0

from making long-term investments, so inflation can have a damaging impact on real economic growth.

In this chapter we first consider the different possible causes of inflation. This will allow us to explain the effects on both inflation and real GDP as the economy reacts to unexpected events ('shocks'). Throughout this discussion we will keep our focus on the different policies that have been used to try to control inflation, including policies that have been tried and subsequently abandoned.

The Causes of Inflation

In normal circumstances competition deters firms from raising prices. So what makes a large proportion of firms in the economy decide to raise prices? Sometimes the answer is obvious. The big peaks in UK inflation were largely due to the sudden rises in global oil prices in 1973 and 1979. Firms which were major oil users raised the prices of their products in order to pass on their increased costs and maintain their profit margins. Where these products were intermediate goods, the firms using them to produce other goods also had to raise their own prices, leading to a wider wave of price rises. This was **cost-push inflation**.

Inflation can also be seen when the economy is booming. In this situation low unemployment makes it hard for employers to recruit the workers they need, and can lead to rapid wage rises as firms try to outbid each other for skilled staff. Firms are again likely to raise their prices in order to maintain their profit margins as their wage bills rise. Indeed, they may see the booming economy as an opportunity to increase their profit margins. This is **demand-pull inflation**.

Inflation can also remain high even after the initial causes have disappeared. To illustrate this, suppose that workers demand a 10 per cent pay rise, and that firms concede this (perhaps because of trade union pressure or fear of losing skilled employees). Firms then

Figure 9.2 The aftermath of hyperinflation
Source: World History Archive/Alamy stock photo

raise their prices by 10 per cent rather than see their profit margins squeezed. If the same occurs throughout the economy, then workers will find that their pay rise has merely matched the 10 per cent rate of overall inflation, leaving them no better off in terms of what they can actually buy with their wages. In response, they are likely to demand an even larger wage increase next year, but this in turn will just lead firms to raise prices, again leaving workers no better off. This is a **wage–price spiral**, and it can lead to sustained—and quite possibly accelerating—inflation. This helps explain why UK inflation remained high throughout the 1970s and into the 1980s, even though unemployment was rising, and long after the immediate impact of the oil price rises had fed through.

One of the lessons of such wage–price spirals is that expectations are important. If workers expect inflation to be high in future, then they are likely to demand large wage rises now, rather than see their real standard of living eroded. If their demands are met, then firms are likely to raise their prices in response. Thus the expectation of future inflation can become reality.

What about the Money Supply?

It may seem odd that we have discussed inflation without mentioning the **money supply**. Surely, as Milton Friedman put it: 'inflation is always and everywhere a monetary phenomenon'? Doesn't this mean that the government can control inflation by limiting the money supply?

Friedman's statement has to be true in one sense because by definition inflation *is* a decline in the value of money. But for the purpose of explaining why inflation arises, the money supply turns out to be a slippery concept, and less useful than might be imagined.

Hyperinflation like that seen in 1920s Germany could not have happened if the government had not printed huge numbers of new banknotes, but the supply of money cannot be the only cause. It is important not to confuse the supply of money with income or with wealth. We are never likely to have as much wealth as we would like, but we are free to hold as much of our wealth as we like in the form of money (we could choose to sell our other assets and store our entire wealth in banknotes underneath our beds). So what would happen if the government suddenly decided to print a vast amount of new cash? Nothing at all. The cash would simply sit unused in a vault, since each of us already holds in cash whatever proportion of our wealth we choose. Other factors must also be at work if this increase in the money supply is to lead to inflation.

A rising money supply might reflect the government running a large fiscal deficit which it finances by printing cash (as seen in the recent hyperinflations in Zimbabwe and Serbia). It would be no surprise if this policy led to sharply increased expectations of future inflation.[2] As we saw in the previous section, such expectations can easily become reality by triggering wage–price spirals. Thus the money supply can certainly be part of the story. Historically, money supply growth has generally tended to rise as inflation rises, but this does not mean that money supply growth necessarily caused the inflation. Ogden Nash made the same point when he playfully suggested that 'wind is caused by the trees waving their branches'. Did I buy a car today because I found an unexpectedly large amount of money in my bank account, or did I decide for completely different reasons to buy a car, and then ensured that I had enough money in my account to pay for it? We need to remember that economics is the study of the choices that people make. Money is just a mechanism for putting these choices into effect.

Another problem is that the **central bank** has no direct control over the money supply. Money is not just coins and banknotes, it is anything that allows economic transactions to take place. Instead of using cash, we can easily use debit cards or cheques to make purchases, so the balances in our bank accounts should also be included as part of the money supply.[3] The central bank is typically responsible for printing all the banknotes in circulation, but this is only a small part of the money supply. We each choose how much of our wealth to keep in our bank accounts—neither the government nor the central bank can influence this directly. Higher interest rates tend to squeeze the money supply by encouraging us to hold less cash and more assets that pay interest, but monetary policy already uses interest rates to affect demand by encouraging saving and discouraging investment. Thus in normal circumstances the money supply does not offer us a separate policy tool for managing the economy.

Confusion is sometimes increased by the terminology that is used. Monetary policy refers to shifting the level of interest rates in order to increase or decrease economic activity. This is what the Bank of England does. **Monetarism** is the belief that control over the money supply has a direct impact on the economy. It does not follow that the Bank of England is full of monetarists.

In the late 1970s and 1980s, successive UK governments announced target ranges for future money supply growth but these targets were rapidly overshot and inflation remained stubbornly high. The repeated failure of this policy saw the government gradually abandon its money supply targets, and few now believe that inflation and the money supply are linked by any reliable relationship.

Box 9.1 Quantitative easing

Over recent years many countries were stimulating their economies as much as was possible using conventional monetary and fiscal policies: interest rates had been cut to near zero and any further increase in government borrowing would run the risk of insolvency. As economic growth remained sluggish, they started to use an unconventional means of stimulating growth: **quantitative easing**.

Under this policy, central banks buy large quantities of the government bonds that have previously been issued (and sometimes other assets). This can be interpreted as a monetarist policy: investors who had owned these bonds were left holding cash instead, so the money supply was clearly increased.

Those who are sceptical of monetarism can instead regard quantitative easing as a means of reducing the cost of long-term borrowing. Central banks typically only have direct control over very short-term (overnight) interest rates, but quantitative easing tends to boost bond prices by making them scarcer (fewer bonds are left in circulation for investors to hold). Higher bond prices make it cheaper for companies to borrow by issuing their own bonds. This in turn is likely to increase investment spending. The exact mechanism involved may remain controversial, but as long as quantitative easing had a positive impact on consumer and investor confidence, this helped achieve the immediate policy objective of increasing demand in the economy.

In sum, trying to control inflation by controlling the money supply faces three key problems: (i) it is not clear how we should measure the money supply; (ii) neither the government nor the central bank has direct control over most of the money supply; (iii) even if they could control the money supply, it is not clear what effect this would have on the economy.

Aggregate Demand and Aggregate Supply

In Chapter 8 we saw how to explain recessions, and in this chapter we have explored the causes of inflation. We can take this analysis one step further by building a more general model of the economy which explains how GDP and inflation respond together to changes in economic conditions. To do this we derive the **aggregate demand** (AD) curve and **aggregate supply** (AS) curve. Like the microeconomic supply and demand curves we met in Chapter 2, these allow us to analyse how GDP and prices adjust as the economy is buffeted by supply and demand shocks.

We saw all the components of demand in Table 7.1 when we measured GDP as total expenditure on final goods: demand from consumers, investment spending, government consumption, and net export demand. The AD curve simply shows total demand in the economy from all these sources at different average price levels.[4]

Back in Chapter 2 we saw that many factors can affect demand for a product. In order to make sense of this we divided these effects into two groups. If the price of the product changes whilst all other factors remain unchanged, then we shift from one point on the demand curve to another. If instead one of these other factors changes (such as household incomes or the price of substitute goods) then we have a demand shock which shifts the whole demand curve. We make the same distinction when we consider the **aggregate demand curve**. In the absence of any wider changes, changes in aggregate output and prices merely shift us from one point on the AD curve to another. A demand shock represents the impact of some other factor which shifts the whole demand curve, for example a boom in the global economy which leads to increased demand for this country's exports. Fiscal and monetary policy changes can be regarded as deliberate demand shocks designed to prevent recessions and inflationary booms—for this reason they are known as **demand side policies**.

However, the level of demand in the economy is only one part of the picture. Will the economy be able to produce this output? The short-run **aggregate supply (AS) curve** is similar to the microeconomic supply curves we saw for specific products in Chapter 2: it tells us whether the economy can increase output without a significant increase in aggregate prices. If the economy is in recession then there will be spare resources (notably unemployed labour) which can be used to increase production without generating inflation. This suggests that the AS curve will be fairly flat. But the productive capacity of the economy is limited. What happens if demand increases further whilst the economy is already working almost flat out? The result is likely to be demand-pull inflation as firms try to raise profit margins and competition for scarce labour pushes wages up. For this reason the short-run AS curve is likely to be fairly flat at low levels of GDP, but progressively steeper as we move to the right.[5]

The usefulness of the AD and AS curves lies in what they tell us about how the economy reacts as conditions change. Suppose that the economy is initially at point A in Figure 9.3, when a positive **aggregate demand shock** (such as a fiscal or monetary policy stimulus) shifts the aggregate demand curve from AD_0 to AD_1. The AS curve is relatively flat here, so the economy will settle at a new equilibrium B with significantly higher real GDP but only slightly higher prices. A further stimulus package could then shift aggregate demand to AD_2, but with the economy already working close to capacity this is likely to result in only a small increase in real GDP and a much larger rise in prices (demand-pull inflation). The steepening AS curve reflects the fact that there is a physical limit on what the economy can produce, although in practice estimating the effective level of spare resources in the economy is likely to be a matter of judgement (see Box 9.2 on the **NAIRU**).

A negative aggregate demand shock is the exact opposite, representing a shift of the AD curve down and to the left. This leads to lower GDP and possibly also falling prices. Recent economic history in many countries was dominated by a massive negative demand shock as investment and consumer spending fell sharply in response to the US housing market crash and the global financial crisis of 2008. GDP fell, and policymakers worried that it might lead to a deflationary spiral, with falling prices making it harder to stimulate the economy.

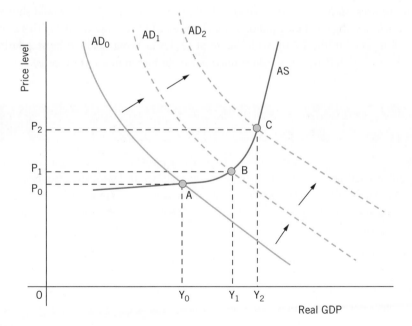

Figure 9.3 Positive aggregate demand shocks

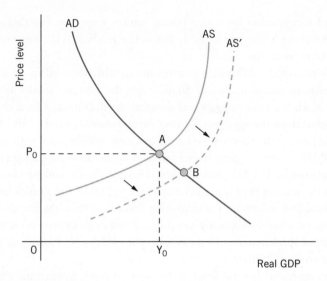

Figure 9.4 Aggregate supply shock

Figure 9.4 shows an **aggregate supply shock**, with the AS curve moving to the right. The economy finds a new equilibrium further down the demand curve, with higher GDP and lower prices. Improved technology can be regarded as a gradual supply shock of this type which leads to higher GDP and cheaper goods. By contrast a sudden rise in import prices (such as the jumps in global oil prices seen in the 1970s) would shift AS to the left, leading to a new equilibrium with lower GDP and higher prices. This is just what happened in the 1970s, with the oil price shocks being followed by **stagflation** (high cost-push inflation even whilst unemployment rose to new record levels).

Box 9.2 How much can the economy produce?

What determines the maximum level of output that the economy can produce without leading to inflation? One intuitive approach is to consider the lowest level of unemployment that can be sustained without resulting in rising inflation (e.g. due to increased wage demands). This is known as the NAIRU: the Non-Accelerating-Inflation Rate of Unemployment.

Sadly, inflation may start to accelerate even whilst significant numbers remain unemployed, because of the following factors.

(i) People vary widely in their skills and motivations. If all potential employees were identical, then the NAIRU could be almost zero, since employers would be willing to hire anyone unemployed. But in practice, the unemployed may not have the skills and characteristics that are attractive to employers, so firms prefer instead to offer higher wages in order to lure better-qualified employees away from other employers. For example, the existence of unemployed steelworkers in one region is of little help to employers looking for software specialists in another part of the country.

(ii) Trade unions may campaign for wage rises for their members (who are already employed) even though the unemployed would be willing to work at lower wages.

(iii) Insufficient competition between firms may lead them to raise prices when demand is high in order to increase their margins.

The most that fiscal and monetary policies can hope to achieve is to push the economy down to the NAIRU. Trying to stimulate the economy more than this will lead to demand-pull inflation. To sustain unemployment rates below this level requires a completely different set of policies. These include changes to education and training to ensure that the unemployed have the skills that employers need; encouraging firms to locate in regions of high unemployment; changing taxes and benefits to ensure that the unemployed have a strong incentive to take available jobs; reducing trade union power and increasing competition between firms. In addition, policies designed to boost investment or research spending aim to increase the amount of GDP produced per employee. These are known as **supply-side policies** because they are designed to shift the AS curve to the right.

In practice economies may be buffeted by a stream of demand and supply shocks. Some of these will originate within the economy, whilst others stem from the international environment (e.g. shifts in commodity prices or demand for exports from a booming global economy). AD and AS curves are a useful tool for understanding the effect of such changes, since they tell us about the impact on both GDP and prices. Demand shocks tend to result in prices and output moving in the same direction (e.g. rising GDP and prices in a boom), whilst supply shocks see them moving in opposite directions (e.g. stagflation).

The Credibility Problem

We saw earlier that in addition to cost-push and demand-pull factors, expectations can play an important role in determining inflation. The wage–price spiral means that if there is a widespread expectation that inflation will be high, then employers are likely to concede large wage rises, with corresponding increases in the prices of their products. Thus the expectation of high inflation can become a reality.

Box 9.3 Immigration and unemployment

The economic principles that we have discussed in this chapter can help shed some light on this fractious debate. The key is to distinguish between microeconomic and macroeconomic effects. We saw in Chapter 5 that we can apply microeconomic supply and demand analysis to a specific labour market such as the market for accountants or plumbers. Just as in any other market, it is perfectly possible that an increase in supply which is not matched by an equivalent increase in demand will push wages down.[6]

It is sometimes claimed that each additional migrant worker automatically increases unemployment by one. This is the 'lump of labour' fallacy. There are two reasons why it is untrue. First, whilst immigration increases the **workforce** (an aggregate supply shock), migrants are also consumers, so their arrival also represents a positive aggregate demand shock. Only if the increased supply outweighs the corresponding demand shock would we expect unemployment to rise as a result. Even then, this would not be the end of the story, since the central bank should be expected to adjust monetary policy in response.

As we have seen (Box 9.2) the central bank should normally be able to push the unemployment rate down to the level of the NAIRU, but not beyond. What effect will migration have on the NAIRU? It depends. If migrants add disproportionately to the supply of types of labour that are already plentiful, and contribute fewer scarce skills, then overall skill shortages could worsen, the NAIRU would be increased, and the Bank of England could not afford to let the aggregate unemployment rate remain low without triggering wage inflation. Alternatively, if migrant workers tend to have skills that are scarce in the existing workforce, then skill shortages would be reduced, allowing the Bank of England to reduce the rate of unemployment further than before without risking rising wage inflation as employers compete for scarce labour.

More generally, journalists and politicians frequently talk of specific numbers of 'jobs created' or 'jobs destroyed' by a particular company or government policy. These claims are often misleading. If a new factory employs 1000 people, will total UK employment rise by 1000? It is unlikely, since this would require that none of these 1000 employees had been employed before the factory opened. Estimating the true impact on employment is a matter of judgement. If the factory employs skilled workers in a region with low unemployment then most of these workers are likely to have been attracted from other employers. A much larger net increase in employment is likely to be achieved if the factory is in an area of high unemployment and employs people with skills that are in excess supply.

Policy-makers have long been aware of this issue. One aim of the money supply targets used in the 1970s and 1980s was that announcing that the money supply would only grow slowly would convince everybody that inflation would also be low. Thus it was hoped that reduced expectations would play a direct role in reducing inflation. This policy failed.

The desire to affect expectations was one reason why the UK joined the European exchange rate mechanism (**ERM**) in 1990. By fixing the value of the pound against the German Deutschmark, policy-makers hoped to signal that UK inflation would have to come down to the same low level as in Germany. This too failed. UK inflation remained higher than in Germany, and with the competitiveness of UK exporters gradually being eroded, people began to doubt that the UK could afford to remain in the ERM. Speculators then started to sell the pound, forcing the UK government to leave the ERM after only two years.

Following these failures, the government decided that rather than targeting inflation indirectly via money supply or exchange rate targets, it would set itself an explicit inflation target. However, it was gradually realized that the government was not trusted to meet its own targets, since people doubted that politicians would be willing to take the unpopular actions (such as raising interest rates immediately before an election) that would sometimes be needed to control inflation. Politicians face an inherent **credibility** problem when it comes to inflation policy.

This realization led to a radical new approach: taking monetary policy out of the hands of politicians. In May 1997 the Bank of England was made responsible for monetary policy. The government gave the Bank of England an explicit target for inflation (currently 2% per annum). The Bank's senior advisers now meet once each month to decide whether they need to change the level of interest rates in order to keep inflation close to this target. This decision is theirs alone, without any influence from the government.

This policy of **central bank independence** has been adopted in almost all developed economies, and has generally been a success. Inflation has remained relatively low partly because of wider factors such as reduced trade union power and increased competition due to the globalization of many industries, but improved policy credibility also appears to have played an important part.

Summary

Inflation can be extremely disruptive, so controlling it is a very important policy goal. In this chapter we explored the different causes of inflation. This allowed us to derive AS and AD curves which help explain how the economy reacts to shocks such as jumps in oil prices or the financial crisis of 2008. We also looked at whether increased demand is likely to lead to higher inflation rather than lower unemployment, and the many different policies governments have used—often with little success—to try to reduce inflation.

More generally, Chapters 7 to 9 have given us a framework which allows us to explain the short-term fluctuations in GDP which can lead to recessions or inflationary booms. In Chapter 10 we briefly consider international trade. In Chapter 11 we move on to examine the very different factors which drive long-term growth, and consider whether these are likely to be sustainable.

CHAPTER 10
INTERNATIONAL ECONOMICS

So far we have discussed exports and imports only briefly. International trade is an important part of the global economy, and an important subject in its own right, but in order to make sense of it we need to start with the more fundamental question of why trade is worthwhile.

The Benefits of Trade

Suppose that, in addition to being a great physicist, Einstein was also a faster and more accurate typist than anyone else. Should he have done his own typing, or should he have hired someone else to do it? This question illustrates a very powerful principle about why trade is worthwhile between individuals, and also between countries.

Table 10.1 shows the simplest possible example of the benefits of trade: two people (Alice and Bob) producing two goods (sweaters and suits). Alice is more productive than Bob in both these tasks. In a full week she can produce 100 sweaters or 20 suits, compared to 24 sweaters or 12 suits for Bob. The middle columns show the output of this simple economy if Alice and Bob each split their time equally between these two tasks.

Table 10.1 Weekly production with different time allocations to different tasks

	Whole week used to produce sweaters	Whole week used to produce suits	Time divided equally between the two products		Specializing in area of comparative advantage	
			sweaters	suits	sweaters	suits
			and		and	
Alice	100	20	50	10	75	5
Bob	24	12	12	6	0	12
			and		and	
Total			**62**	**16**	**75**	**17**

The right-hand section of the table shows how much the economy could produce if Bob specializes entirely in making suits, whilst Alice spends 75 per cent of her time making sweaters. The economy has become more productive, since it now produces more of both goods than before (75 sweaters and 17 suits). How is this possible?

Alice is better at both tasks (she has an **absolute advantage** in both), but she is much better than Bob at making sweaters, and only slightly better at suits: she has a **comparative advantage** in producing sweaters. This can be seen when we consider the opportunity costs involved. In the time taken to produce one suit, she could have produced five sweaters. By contrast, in the (longer) time taken for Bob to produce one suit he could have produced only two sweaters. The benefits of trade come from the difference in these opportunity costs. If Bob produces two fewer sweaters he can produce one more suit. Alice can produce one less suit, but then five more sweaters. These small

Box 10.1 The trade balance and the current account

We saw in Table 7.1 that the value of imports into the UK exceeded the value of UK exports, implying a UK **trade deficit** of around 2.1 per cent of GDP. Additional items (e.g. the interest paid on assets such as UK government bonds which have been bought by non-UK residents) mean that the total **current account deficit** is larger at 4.3 per cent.[1] To fund this deficit the UK must borrow (or run down its overseas assets).

Such deficits are not necessarily a bad thing. Just as it might be perfectly sensible for people to borrow money at some stages in their lives (e.g. to pay for higher education), it can make perfect sense for a country to run a deficit if the borrowed funds are used to invest in productive capacity which will boost future GDP and exports (in particular since this will help the country subsequently to repay what it has borrowed). By contrast, a deficit which is used to fund consumption is more likely to lead to problems.

A current account deficit represents borrowing either by the government (a fiscal deficit) or the private sector (firms and households), and it will be sustainable only for as long as international lenders are confident that their loans will be repaid. If the total amount of debt becomes excessive, then lenders may decide to stop lending, which could lead to significant economic instability, for example through a sharp fall in the exchange rate. For this reason a large current account deficit raises the question of whether the country involved is following sustainable economic policies.

The gradual removal of government controls on international borrowing/lending and the development of the international financial system have made it easier for one country to borrow from another. Some economies (notably China, Japan, and Germany) have now been running current account surpluses for many years, whilst others (including the USA and the UK) have been running corresponding deficits. Many economists are worried that this situation is unsustainable, and is likely to lead to substantial economic volatility at some stage in the future.[2]

changes would leave them producing three more sweaters than before. Even though Bob is less productive at both tasks than Alice, he has a comparative advantage in making suits, and the output of our simple economy increases if Alice and Bob each specialize in their field of comparative advantage.

Table 10.1 shows that **specialization** increases total economic output—it is a positive sum game. It does not tell us whether Alice or Bob actually gains more from this (this depends on the prices at which sweaters and suits are traded—the 'terms of trade'). However, it should make both parties better off, since neither is being forced to trade: they could each reject any proposed deal which left them worse off than in the absence of trade. This is the basic argument for allowing free trade: that trade only ever takes place if both parties find it advantageous.[3]

Trade takes place between countries for pretty much the same reasons as trade between people. Trade allows specialization, and this can be beneficial if some countries are comparatively better at producing some things than others (regardless of whether trading partners have higher or lower productivity than each other in absolute terms). This comparative advantage might be due to their natural resources, or because one country has invested time and effort to become productive in a particular field.

Even if Einstein had been a slightly better typist than anyone else, he was still a far better physicist than he was typist. His comparative advantage was in physics, so it was very beneficial for him to specialize in physics and hire someone else to do his typing. The opportunity cost of each hour Einstein spent typing was an hour he could have spent on physics. His talent in physics made these hours too valuable to waste on typing.

Exchange Rates

International trade frequently requires one currency to be exchanged for another. For example, a US company importing goods from the UK may need to pay for these in British pounds. Even if the British firm presents its invoice in US dollars, it is likely to convert the dollars it receives into pounds in order to pay its workers and suppliers. Either way, dollars need to be exchanged for pounds. This is done in the **foreign exchange markets** (often known simply as FX markets).

Some people will want to exchange dollars for pounds, whilst others want to exchange pounds for dollars. The market price will adjust until supply equals demand. The price in this market is known as the **exchange rate**, and represents the amount of one currency that must be paid in order to buy a given amount of another. There are many different currencies so there are many exchange rates, such as the number of US dollars that you can buy with one British pound, or the number of Japanese yen that you can buy with one euro.

These are markets like any other. Most FX trading is electronic, but you are also participating in the FX market when you go on a foreign holiday and exchange some of your own currency for cash in the currency of the country you are visiting, allowing you to pay for things whilst you are away.[4]

We discussed exports and imports briefly in Chapters 7 and 8. Exports from a country such as the UK represent additional demand for the products of UK firms: an injection of additional spending into the UK economy, just like government spending and investment. Conversely, imports are a withdrawal of expenditure (UK household income which is not spent on the products of UK firms), just like taxes and savings. Thus in principle we have three injection/withdrawal pairs which can affect overall demand in the economy:

1. government spending and taxation (which can be adjusted as part of *fiscal policy*);

2. investment and savings flows (which will be sensitive to *monetary policy*—for example, lower interest rates tend to encourage investment and discourage saving);

3. exports and imports.

Just as shifts in interest rates tend to alter the balance between investment and saving, so shifts in the exchange rate tend to alter the balance between exports and imports. For example, a shift in the exchange rate between the US dollar and British pound could make it more expensive for UK consumers to buy goods that were produced in the USA, and correspondingly cheaper for US consumers to buy goods produced in the UK.[5] Imports into the UK from the USA (a withdrawal of spending from the UK economy) would then tend to fall and exports from the UK to the USA (an injection of spending into the UK economy) would tend to rise. Both these effects would stimulate the UK economy.

This suggests that in principle shifting the exchange rate could be used as a tool of macroeconomic policy just like shifting interest rates, but most are **floating exchange rates**, which are determined by supply and demand for these currencies in the FX markets. Governments have no direct control over these exchange rates, just as they have no direct control over share prices.

Floating exchange rates may vary in response to economic developments in the countries involved, but they also react to political news and many other factors. Even supposed experts have an extremely poor track record in trying to forecast exchange rate movements! An unexpected shift in interest rates by the central bank does tend to affect the country's exchange rate, but interest rates are already used for monetary policy, so this doesn't represent an additional tool for adjusting economic demand. Far from being a useful policy tool, shifts in the exchange rate tend to be an unwelcome complication that central banks need to take into account when deciding what level of interest rates is appropriate.[6]

Rather than accepting this unwanted volatility, some governments have tried to run **fixed exchange rates**, where the government sets a target level or range for the exchange rate, and promises to buy or sell its currency in the FX market in order to keep the exchange rate at this level. The UK's short-lived membership of the ERM (discussed in Chapter 9) was one example of this. Similarly, many Asian countries used to fix their exchange rates against the US dollar, but in 1997/98 massive speculative currency flows forced most to abandon this policy, resulting in substantial economic volatility. Following this experience, the majority of governments now accept floating exchange rates.[7]

Even where governments can directly influence their exchanges rates, this may be controversial. For example, in a global recession one government might wish to weaken its currency in order to boost its **net exports**, but this would be a beggar-your-neighbour policy, since its trading partners would find that their currencies have appreciated correspondingly, thus reducing demand in their economies. Allegations of such currency manipulation can be a source of international tension: some US politicians argue that China has been keeping its currency at an artificially cheap exchange rate and thus 'pricing US workers out of jobs'.

Summary

International trade has grown massively over recent years. In itself this is welcome, since it allows each country to specialize in producing the goods and services in which it is relatively efficient. This should be mutually beneficial to the countries involved. However, international trade brings some complications:

- Exchange rate movements can be an unwelcome source of economic volatility. Central banks need to take such shifts into account when setting monetary policy.

- Exports are an increasingly important component of aggregate demand in most countries. This means that even without exchange rate volatility, one economy can be affected by a reduction of demand in another. For example, even countries which were not directly affected by the 2008 financial crisis were affected by the reduction in world trade that it caused.

- The need to fund current account deficits has led to increased amounts being borrowed/lent between countries. This was an underlying factor leading to the 2008 crisis, and it may cause further instability in future.

CHAPTER 11
GROWTH AND WELFARE

We saw in Chapter 8 that short-term GDP fluctuations are mainly caused by shifts in aggregate demand (demand shocks), and that 'demand side' fiscal and monetary policies can be used to combat these shifts. By contrast, long-term GDP growth has been driven by a gradual shift of the aggregate supply curve to the right. The result has been a rise in GDP that has dramatically improved the material living standards of successive generations.[1]

Three key factors have driven this long-term supply shift: the size of the **labour force**, the amount of capital used in the production process, and the technology which turns these labour and capital inputs into useful output. Let us consider each of these in turn.

UK population has almost doubled since 1885, but real GDP has grown much more rapidly, resulting in a sevenfold increase in real GDP per person over this period.[2]

The capital used in producing GDP takes many forms, such as land, natural resources, and the physical infrastructure of roads, buildings, and factories. We should also include **human capital**. For example, spending time and money on education and training is likely to boost our future productivity, so this is a valuable investment just as much as a physical asset is. Measuring the total productive capital of the UK economy is not easy, but it is clear that this has played only a modest part in long-term GDP growth. After all, the fourteen-fold increase in real GDP shown in Figure 11.1 has not been achieved by installing fourteen times as many steam engines and cotton mills as before. We now use very different techniques to produce things that were not previously possible. Many of the jobs we do and the products we buy would have been unknown in the nineteenth century. The key driver of long-term real growth in GDP per person has been this improved technology.[3]

The introduction of new technology has sometimes been vigorously opposed by those whose livelihoods depend on technology which is becoming obsolete. However, the long-term benefits of this new technology have been huge. If the associated shifts in employment had been successfully resisted, then many people would still be employed as coopers, wheelwrights, and tallow renderers. But our economies would be much less productive, losing us many of the material benefits we currently enjoy.

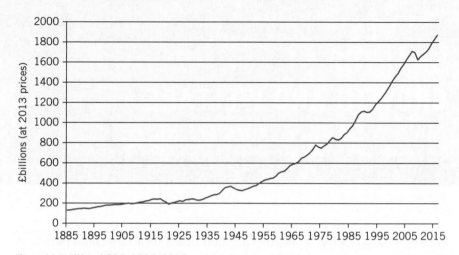

Figure 11.1 UK real GDP, 1885–2016

Source: 'A Millennium of Macroeconomic Data', R. Thomas and N. Dimsdale, Bank of England (2017), constructed using estimates from the following sources: Andersson and Lennard (2017), Broadberry et al. (2015), Feinstein (1972), Geary and Stark (2004, 2015), Mitchell (1988), Sefton and Weale (1995), Solomou and Weale (1991)

What can governments do to encourage innovation and the rapid adoption by firms of the best available technologies? There is a broad consensus about some of the factors that are important. A legal system which gives well-defined property rights allows long-term investments to be undertaken without fear that the benefits will be taken by someone else. Infrastructure such as transport and telecommunications is also important, as is a healthy and well-educated workforce. Wider cultural and political values may also play a role in determining how readily institutions adapt to change. Beyond this, there is debate about measures such as tax incentives for research and development, and more generally about whether government intervention is beneficial (in encouraging

Box 11.1 The end of work?

Ever since the Industrial Revolution there have been forecasts that new technology would destroy jobs and lead to mass unemployment. In fact technology has created as many new jobs as it replaced. Pessimistic forecasts have been common because it is easy to identify existing jobs that are likely to be displaced by new technology, but much harder to identify the new types of employment that will be created. For example, it was relatively easy fifty years ago to forecast that automation would reduce employment on factory production lines, but hard to predict that significant numbers of people would now be employed as website developers or personal trainers. Looking ahead, it is tempting to forecast that there must inevitably come a point at which artificial intelligence results in machines which are better than humans at all jobs. However, the track record of excessively pessimistic forecasts in the past should make us wary of jumping to this conclusion too soon.

the development of new industries) or counterproductive (in producing expensive white elephants).[4]

Developing new technology is a slow and expensive process, but transferring existing technology to other countries can be much quicker and cheaper. The most spectacular economic growth has been in economies which initially lagged behind advanced countries in terms of GDP per person, for example if they were still largely agricultural, or used outdated and inefficient technology. From this low starting point, they could adopt the very latest technology, leapfrogging the now-obsolete technologies (such as steam power) which other economies had installed as they industrialized earlier. Real GDP growth in the range of 5–10 per cent per annum was recorded by 'Asian tiger' economies such as Singapore, Hong Kong, South Korea, and Taiwan as they industrialized following World War II, and more recently by China.[5] To put this into perspective, a growth rate of 7 per cent per annum implies that real GDP will double every ten years! By comparison, real UK GDP growth has averaged 2 per cent since 1885, although even this relatively modest rate of growth has been sufficient to alter living standards dramatically over this period.

This seems to suggest that we can all look forward to improved technology making us ever richer and happier. However, there are four key challenges to this: (i) Why are some economies still stuck in poverty? (ii) Are high levels of real GDP sustainable? (iii) Will income inequality inevitably increase within developed economies? (iv) How much happier has increased material wealth made us?

Why Are Some Economies Still Stuck in Poverty?

Economic growth has dramatically reduced the proportion of the world's population living in extreme poverty,[6] but even though the potential for catch-up is huge, some countries have remained stuck at relatively low levels of GDP per person. Lack of natural resources does not generally appear to be the reason. Some economies have become rich through their mineral wealth (notably oil), but others have achieved this with very limited natural resources (for example Japan, Israel, Singapore, and Hong Kong). Conversely, many poor countries in sub-Saharan Africa have very significant mineral wealth.[7]

Bad government appears to be a key factor. Quality of government is strongly correlated with economic development. War is a major cause of poverty, but smaller-scale corruption, crime, and violence also slow growth not only through the cost of the resources that are destroyed or misappropriated but also because of their effect on incentives. The absence of reliable legal rights means that the most effective way to get rich is not by creating wealth, but by taking it from someone else. Excessive government regulation can also result in numerous government permits being required for even simple business tasks. Such bureaucracy also encourages corruption as officials offer shortcuts through the process—at a price. Bad government can also lead to macroeconomic instability via periodic inflation or chronic government deficits which further deter investment.[8]

Inappropriate policies can also make it harder to benefit from the innate gains from trade (via the comparative advantages we discussed in Chapter 10), for example because of a mistaken emphasis on self-sufficiency, or by imposing a level of central planning which impedes growth. This can be seen when changes in government policy remove previous constraints on growth. China's spectacular growth only started after economic reforms, beginning in the late 1970s, began to move the economy away from rigid central planning, allowing a larger element of market forces.

However, blaming bad government does not imply that there are easy solutions, since bad government is at least in part the result of poverty and instability as well as the cause. Many of the other problems faced by the poorest countries are also vicious circles: removing the impediments which prevent higher economic growth is difficult without higher economic growth. Some technologies are rendered unviable by a lack of basic infrastructure (such as reliable transport infrastructure and electricity supply) or a labour force whose effectiveness has been undermined by poor education and health problems. Developing countries may suffer a 'brain drain' as those with valuable skills leave for higher pay in richer countries. Population growth also tends to be high in low-income countries, placing further strain on resources. Large families leave few resources for educating these children, and girls in particular are often undereducated. An undeveloped financial sector can be an additional constraint on growth: microfinance schemes which make small loans (often to women) have recorded some notable successes.

Beyond this, there is continuing debate about the best policies for encouraging economic growth. Understanding the complex and interrelated reasons why some countries lag behind is the central question of **development economics**.

Sustainability

Let us start with some good news. Back in 1798 Thomas Malthus forecast that our finite agricultural resources would inevitably fail to keep up with exponential rates of population growth, leading to periodic mass starvation. This line of thinking has remained popular. However, agricultural production has improved so rapidly (the 'green revolution') that we have not seen global starvation even though the population has grown to around 7.5 billion from only 2.5 billion in 1950 (and around 1 billion in 1800). The rate of population growth has been slowing as birth rates decline, and is expected to continue to slow, with world population reaching 10 billion around 2055.[9] This is an astonishing number in some respects, but the 33 per cent further growth from current levels is modest compared to the trebling seen since 1950.

Food is plentiful in developed economies. This can be seen in the fact that it is comparatively cheap. Food now accounts for only around 16 per cent of spending by the average UK household (and this includes eating out in restaurants). Indeed, food is so cheap that we waste a significant proportion of what is produced. This waste naturally seems obscene, but it also gives us a buffer for coping with any future agricultural problems, since if food were to become scarcer, and hence more expensive, we can be pretty confident that we would stop wasting so much.

Population growth exacerbates environmental problems and makes it harder to raise living standards in some of the poorest countries. Almost 800 million people around the world are still undernourished[10] and childhood malnutrition can have serious and lasting impact. This is a massive human tragedy, but it is not the inevitable global starvation that had been widely forecast. The world has produced enough food, but hunger remains where poverty means that people do not have access to it. Major famines have often been the result of war or political upheaval which has disrupted local production and distribution.[11]

There have also been many forecasts of the imminent depletion of mineral resources, but when resources become scarcer they rise in price, giving a strong incentive to find new sources of these materials or substitutes which can fulfil the same functions. Some commodity prices have risen, whilst others have fallen, but overall averages have shown little sustained change over the last fifty years.[12] This is not to say that finite resources won't be depleted at some stage, but forecasts based on simple extrapolation of recent extraction rates have tended to be very wide of the mark because they assumed that resources dwindle to zero without taking account of any change in incentives as prices shift. It would be foolish to take our future supplies of food or raw materials for granted, but thus far this has generally been a success story as our economies have coped with massive increases in demand.

Beyond this, we need to make an important distinction. There are some problems that people have a strong incentive to try to prevent. This generally includes avoiding shortages of food or other commodities, since it is likely to be very profitable to supply goods which are becoming scarce (and hence expensive). However, there are other areas in which nervousness about the future seems entirely justified, especially when caused by externalities such as pollution, or the overuse of shared resources. We saw the incentives involved when we discussed the prisoner's dilemma in Chapter 4. Everyone may be well aware of the need for action, but the best strategy for each individual decision-maker may be to free ride and hope that everyone else takes care of the problem. Past experience has shown that people can make very bad decisions in such situations.

The biggest such problem is global warming. The consensus of scientific opinion is that human CO_2 emissions are already affecting the climate globally, and this effect is set to increase in future.[13] The need for international agreement to limit carbon emissions has been clear, but reaching any such agreement has been very slow, even assuming agreement remains effective. This is the all-too-predictable outcome of the prisoner's dilemma.

Destroying my own resources via mismanagement or overuse would be stupid. By contrast, overusing a resource which I share with other people is selfish and irresponsible, but entirely rational. The prisoner's dilemma can be seen in many of our toughest environmental problems, including threats to food supply: the overuse of common water supplies, atmospheric pollution, overgrazing, destruction of the rainforest, and overfishing. In each of these cases the challenge is to reach an effective collective agreement, overcoming the incentive each of us has to free ride.

Inequality

There has been some convergence in the average levels of GDP per person seen in different countries, since growth in developing countries has generally been more rapid than in richer countries. However, as discussed earlier in this chapter, some poor countries have failed to achieve this rapid growth.

The distribution of incomes *within* each country is a different matter. Inequality within economies such as the UK and the USA has risen. Reduced transport costs and improved communication technology have resulted in increased **globalization**. This has increased the number of workers in high-income economies who are now competing with workers in poorer economies. This trend has seen not only increased imports of manufactured goods from lower-wage economies, but also the relocation of services such as call centres.

The impact of globalization in higher-income economies has been reinforced by the more general impact of technological change, which has reduced the demand for manual and unskilled labour, whilst the new jobs created by this technology have typically demanded higher skill levels. This has increased wage differentials (as well as creating a small number of technology billionaires). New technology and increased international trade have tended to increase average levels of GDP per person, but this will not have benefited everyone. The losers have been those in jobs which have been replaced by automation, or who cannot compete with much cheaper overseas labour.

Governments in developed economies can try to soften this blow in two ways. They can provide training to help people shift into jobs in different fields. They can also reduce inequality directly by redistributing income. Free markets are not a take-it-or-leave-it choice. Governments often accept the benefits of trade, whilst also seeking to alleviate the undesirable side effects within their economies. Specifically, governments often play a substantial role in redistributing income by levying **progressive taxes** (under which the better-off pay a higher proportion of their incomes as tax) and paying benefits to ensure at least a minimum standard of living for the poorest. It is generally accepted that there is some degree of trade-off here. The incentive to invest or to work hard is reduced if it is perceived that a large proportion of the benefits will be taken in tax. Thus dividing the economic pie more equally would tend to make the pie as a whole slightly smaller. However, the extent of this trade-off is widely debated, and the appropriate degree to which governments should aim to reduce economic inequality is rightly regarded as a political value judgement rather than a purely economic decision.

Figure 11.2 shows the redistributive effect of the UK tax and benefit system. The poorest 20 per cent receive 4 per cent of original incomes, but 10 per cent of incomes after tax and benefits. Conversely, the top 20 per cent receive 48 per cent of original incomes,

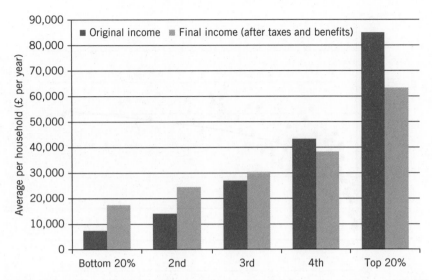

Figure 11.2 The effect of taxes and benefits on UK household incomes (financial year 2015/16)
Source: Adapted from data from Office for National Statistics licensed under Open Government Licence v.3.0

but 37 per cent following taxes and benefits. Thus the UK tax and benefit system has a significant impact, but substantial inequality remains. Inequality has increased markedly in most developed economies in recent years. For example, the poorest 40 per cent of the US population has seen no increase in average real income since the 1970s. Instead economic growth has overwhelmingly benefited those at the top of the distribution.[14] Looking forward, a key question is what degree of inequality will be considered politically acceptable if the underlying forces of globalization and improved technology continue to increase the inequality of pre-tax incomes.

How Happy Are We?

Long-term growth in GDP per person has dramatically improved average living standards in material terms, but this has not made us as happy as might have been expected.

Figure 11.3 shows the results of surveys which asked people in a wide range of different countries how happy they were. At very low levels of per capita GDP the trend is upwards: an increase in real GDP is associated with a substantial rise in average happiness. People who lack basic facilities and are uncertain about whether they will be able to feed themselves or their families are likely to become considerably happier as GDP per person increases. But at a relatively modest level the trend flattens off, with the richest countries showing average happiness levels only slightly higher than middle-income counties.[15] Consistent with this, real per capita UK GDP has more than doubled since 1970, yet the proportion of people describing themselves as happy has risen only very slightly. The same is true for other developed economies.

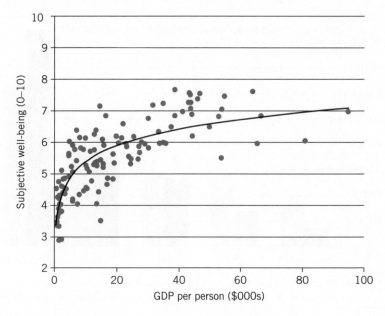

Figure 11.3 Happiness and GDP per person for different countries
Source: J. Helliwell, R. Layard, and J. Sachs, World Happiness Report 2017 (New York: Sustainable Development Solutions Network, 2017)

This curve is not entirely surprising. In Chapter 3 we argued that we should expect diminishing marginal utility as we increase our consumption of most goods. Correspondingly, Figure 11.3 shows every extra $1000 of income bringing a smaller and smaller increase in reported happiness. In any case, the curve had to level out at some point, since the highest possible level of happiness in these surveys is 10. Nevertheless, it is sobering to see how rapidly happiness flattens out as countries become richer.

Analysis of the corresponding data for individuals shows that we tend to become happier following a sudden increase in our incomes, but this extra happiness tends to diminish as we start taking our new income for granted. We are also very sensitive to how our income compares with other peoples': knowing that many people are richer than us makes us unhappy. We appear to compare our current income with easy benchmarks such as what we earned in the recent past, and what others earn now, but we find it much more difficult to keep a longer-term perspective. Being transported back 200 years would probably be a very powerful reminder of how much we should value many things that we currently take for granted, such as indoor plumbing, modern medicine, and dentistry. We are all likely to have been told to 'count our blessings'. This is good advice, but we appear to find it very difficult to do.

The data also show that factors other than income have an important impact on happiness, such as good health, good relationships with friends and family, and feeling part of a community in which we feel safe and supported and in which we can trust people. Those who feel that their lives have meaning or purpose also tend to be happier. Consistent with this, unemployment has a negative impact on happiness which goes well beyond the impact it has on income.[16] Giving money away also tends to make us happier than spending the same amount on ourselves.[17]

There is clearly much more to happiness than simply consuming as much as possible. However, this does not mean that it was a mistake to make the very simple assumptions about consumer behaviour that we used in Chapters 2 and 3. It is a matter of using the right model for the job. Our earlier simple assumptions gave us a simple model that is generally perfectly adequate to explain how consumers tend to react to rising prices, rising incomes, or the availability of substitutes. More complex models are likely to be needed to explain more important life decisions.

However, happiness theory raises important questions for us as individuals. For example, do we sometimes overestimate the extent to which increased consumption will make us happier? This might be an understandable mistake, given that £20 billion is spent in the UK each year on advertising which aims to convince us to buy things that we otherwise would not. Government policy might also have a significant impact on non-income factors which affect happiness. For this reason happiness theory is being taken increasingly seriously by governments around the world. For example, the UK Office for National Statistics and the OECD now produce estimates of national well-being as well as GDP.

Summary

This chapter has dealt very briefly with a number of extremely important issues. Entire books have been written on each one! Our short introduction to these topics has shown:

- Technology has been the key driver of the long-term growth in GDP per person which has transformed material living standards.

- Some countries have failed to share in this growth, and remain stuck in poverty. Analysing the reasons for this is the central challenge of development economics.

- The green revolution has dramatically improved agricultural yields, allowing population growth without the global starvation that had been forecast. Important challenges remain, mainly in areas where our incentives are misaligned, in particular where the prisoner's dilemma gives us an incentive to neglect or overuse shared resources.

- Happiness theory is an exciting new field which digs deeper into the factors which make us happy as individuals, and policies which might contribute to a happy society.

CHAPTER 12

SUMMARY: A SHORT HISTORY OF MACROECONOMIC POLICY

Macroeconomics is a relatively young science. It has evolved rapidly as situations arose which could not be adequately explained by existing theory. It is also a very applied science, so one neat way to summarize the theory that we have covered in the second half of this book is to look at the different macroeconomic policies that have been used.

Until the 1930s there was no such field as macroeconomics, since it was assumed that the whole economy could be explained using microeconomic principles. The aggregate labour market was regarded as just like any other market, so unemployment (excess supply of labour) was expected to be temporary since wages would naturally tend to fall until this excess disappeared. The best policy was thought to be for the government to allow the market to adjust without government intervention (a policy known as 'laissez-faire').

The Great Depression showed that this classical model of the economy could be very misleading. Instead, the Keynesian model argued that aggregate demand depends on incomes and incomes depend on aggregate demand. This explained how the economy could get stuck in long periods of high unemployment. It also suggested that fiscal policy could offer a solution, since if demand from the private sector was falling the government might be able to offset this by spending more or cutting taxes. Fiscal policy was used fairly successfully in stabilizing the economy from 1945 until the end of the 1960s.

The 1970s raised a new challenge: inflation which persisted even when the immediate causes (cost push and demand pull) had passed. Monetarism tried to cure this and failed. The UK's membership of the ERM (1990–2) failed spectacularly. Inflation was mainly reduced by the painful recessions of the early 1980s and 1990s, but since then an independent Bank of England following a clear inflation target has generally succeeded in keeping UK inflation low. Central bank independence has now been adopted in almost all developed economies as a means of avoiding the credibility problem that arises when politicians run monetary policy.

The taming of inflation led to talk of a 'great moderation' as these improved macroeconomic policies were believed to have greatly reduced economic volatility. In particular, UK Chancellor of the Exchequer Gordon Brown claimed that his policies would avoid the previous pattern of 'boom and bust'. The 2008 global financial crisis showed that these claims were premature. This crisis was caused by information and incentive problems (as discussed in Chapter 5) and the resulting collapse in confidence triggered a shift from high consumer and investment spending to very low spending. Fiscal and monetary policy were used to boost demand (central banks slashed interest rates and many governments increased spending) and a new stimulus policy was added (quantitative easing).

What does the future hold? Chapter 11 discussed some of the key challenges: ensuring sustainability; increasing economic growth and reducing poverty in the poorest countries; addressing the increased inequality within richer countries; and encouraging the wider non-material factors which promote happiness. However, there are also likely to be less predictable problems. Macroeconomics has come a long way, and has given us a range of policies which can—at least some of the time—address major problems. However, it is still an evolving field, and it is likely to continue to develop in response to unexpected new policy challenges.

CHAPTER 13
CONCLUSION

In this final chapter it is time to take stock. To start with, we can now dismiss some common misperceptions about economics. First, we have seen that economics is not about money—it is about the choices people make. We considered money in Chapter 9 and found it to be a surprisingly unhelpful concept. Second, economics does not imply a belief that free markets are always best. We started in Chapter 1 with the astonishing fact that market economies work as well as they do, but Chapter 4 identified a number of market failures where government intervention might improve things (although badly designed policies could easily make things worse).

It is worth comparing economics with other sciences. In this book we have discussed different economic models. Other sciences refer instead to *theories*, but the concept is the same: a theory is put forward to explain the available facts. If new information becomes available which is inconsistent with this theory, then the theory is rejected and replaced with another. This is the fundamental scientific method. In physics, quantum theory was introduced to explain new experimental results which were inconsistent with existing theories. Similarly, the great depression resulted in the classical model of unemployment being replaced by the Keynesian model. Physicists can conduct experiments which measure results under controlled conditions. This is a luxury which is not available in macroeconomics, where new economic data are only revealed gradually as history unfolds, but economic theory will continue to adapt to what new data tell us.

Economics is also a very applied science. It seeks not only to understand how things work, but also to help them work better. We have covered many policy issues in this book. Politicians also love to deploy economic theory in support of their views. Economics is unlikely to make political disagreements disappear, but it can help clarify why people disagree. Sometimes it is because people have fundamentally different models of how the economy works, but more often disagreement stems from different judgements about the key facts used in applying these theories: for example, tax policy depends on a judgement about the extent to which progressive taxation will deter people from taking paid employment or working harder. Similarly, environmental policies depend on estimates of the size of the externalities involved. Economics can help identify the underlying sources of these disagreements and hopefully encourage more evidence-based policies.

Disagreements can also be the result of value judgements, such as the extent to which we should be willing to accept lower GDP as a consequence of distributing this GDP more equally. Such value judgements are a matter of politics rather than economics, but economics can help make more informed policy choices by distinguishing between value judgements and judgements of fact.

We have come a long way in this deliberately short book. To do this we have tried to focus on the key insights and present them as intuitively as possible. Please forgive us where we have had to cover important issues in just a few pages (in particular, the long-term challenges identified in Chapter 11). We have given sources for further reading in the notes for each chapter.

We hope that this book has helped give you a better understanding of how the economy works. Economics is an evolving science which can help us understand the choices we face; the behaviour that we see around us every day; the behavioural biases which might lead us to make bad decisions; the policy issues that face us now and the challenges that will face future generations.

In particular, we hope that we have convinced you that economics does not need to be mathematical or complex. Economics is too important to be left only to the mathematically minded.

We hope that you have enjoyed this book.

ENDNOTES

Chapter 2

1 All the price elasticities in Figure 2.1 are actually likely to be negative (since an increased price results in a decrease in demand), but in common parlance goods whose demand is sensitive to price are generally referred to (as we do here) as having greater price elasticity, when strictly speaking these elasticities are more negative. Our experience as consumers allows us to make an educated guess about these elasticities, but deriving specific numerical estimates is harder. Firms can use consumer questionnaires, or track demand over periods when prices change. This information is valuable, which is one reason why supermarkets distribute loyalty cards which allow them to track cardholders' purchases over time. Some estimates of elasticities of demand for food items are available in Richard Lipsey and Alec Chrystal, *Economics* 14th edition (Oxford: Oxford University Press, 2018), table 3.2, and the surrounding text offers estimates for some other products.

2 Note that for some goods the elasticity of demand may be greater in the long term than the short term, since consumers may need time to adjust fully. For example, if I have oil-fired central heating, then a rise in the price of oil may initially have little impact on my consumption, since my immediate choices are either using oil or being cold. In the longer term, if the higher price is sustained, I have other options, such as converting to gas central heating. Conversely, the elasticity of demand for durable goods such as cars may be higher in the short term since it is easy to delay replacing such goods for a while. For a discussion of these points, see Lipsey and Chrystal, *Economics* 14th edition, chapter 3.

3 By contrast, demand for sports cars as a whole is likely to be less price-elastic since if the price of all sports cars rose, then consumers would be faced with alternatives which are not close substitutes. It is not entirely clear what these alternatives would be, since it is not clear why people buy sports cars. Are they a means of transport or a status symbol? For many consumers the alternative is likely to be another type of car, but for some it might be an entirely different status symbol such as a yacht.

4 Some markets are indeed local, such as where long travel would be inconvenient: bulky and perishable goods, a restaurant meal, or a haircut. Others are clearly global, such as for crude oil and other major commodities.

5 Note that we could equally well describe the change in Figure 2.5 as the supply curve shifting up rather than to the left. The new curve tells us that at any given price producers will supply fewer eggs than before (left), and equivalently that they will only be willing to supply any given quantity at a higher price than before (up). Either way, this would clearly be an unwelcome change for consumers. Just as for demand curves, a relatively flat supply curve reflects a high elasticity of supply (a small price increase would trigger a large increase

in supply). In practice this elasticity is likely to be greater in the **long run** (when firms have been able to fully adjust their production processes) than in the **short run**.

6 Exactly how the new price is set depends on the structure of the industry. A firm which has no competitors (a *monopoly*) can choose for itself the prices it will charge in future. In other industries the exact price set by each firm will depend on what competing firms charge, but any one of these firms can anticipate that excess supply now is likely to lead to lower prices in future. We consider monopoly and competition in Chapter 3. More generally, in most markets firms set the price of the good and then see how much consumers are willing to buy at this price, but in a few there will be an element of negotiation between buyer and seller. For more detail on this see the discussion of administered and auction prices in the final section of chapter 2 of Lipsey and Chrystal, *Economics* 14th edition.

7 For more in-depth discussion of the examples used here and others, see the case studies at the end of chapters 2, 3, and 6 of Lipsey and Chrystal, *Economics* 14th edition.

8 The consumers who continue to drink coffee will tend to be those who strongly prefer coffee to alternative beverages. Those with less strong preferences will tend to switch. This seems fair, since this year's reduced supply of coffee will then tend to be consumed by those who enjoy it most. But the remaining coffee will also tend to go to the rich, who are happy to continue to buy it at its new higher price even if they only marginally prefer coffee over cheaper alternatives. More enthusiastic, but poorer, coffee drinkers may be amongst those who shift to other beverages. A desirable property of markets is that they allocate goods to those who tend to value them most. A less desirable property is that the preferences of the rich are given greater weight than the preferences of the poor. This has been described as markets being 'one pound, one vote', in contrast to the democratic 'one person, one vote'.

Chapter 3

1 Consumers clearly don't perform this calculation exactly as we have set out here, but they do ask themselves 'should I consume more milk, or are there other products that would give me more enjoyment for the same money?'. The model we describe here captures this key aspect of our decision-making, so it is a 'wrong but useful' model of consumer behaviour. In particular, it generates predictions which are consistent with the behaviour that we actually observe: that consumers tend to buy more of a product if its price falls.

2 An exclusivity agreement is likely to prevent other promoters from arranging additional concerts in the area by the same performer. These competing promoters can arrange concerts by other performers, but fans are likely to regard these as poor substitutes for seeing their favourite.

3 Undercutting my competitors is likely to squeeze my profit margins unsustainably low (unless for some reason my firm's costs are lower than theirs). The demand curve for the industry as a whole slopes downwards, so any increase in my output will push prices down a bit, but this effect will be tiny if my firm is just one of a very large number of similar firms in the industry. Thus even if I dramatically increase my production (for example doubling my output), the effect on total industry production will be negligible, so in practice I should act as if the curve was flat.

4 The same applies to airline tickets, but is complicated by continual adjustment of prices as the airline gets a better idea of whether a particular flight is popular. By contrast, train discounts are simpler and prices are typically sold according to fixed rules which only very approximately discriminate between popular and unpopular travel times.

5 A secure monopoly requires a **barrier to entry** which stops new competitors, such as a patent which forbids any other firm from selling a similar product, or factors which would make it very expensive to enter this industry. One example is the patent protection given to newly developed pharmaceuticals, which gives the producer a monopoly for up to 20 years. This clearly has a large impact on consumers, but this is a deliberate policy trade-off, since without it firms would have little incentive to develop new drugs. See case study 3 in chapter 7 of Lipsey and Chrystal, *Economics* 14th edition.

Chapter 4

1 In the UK many of these industries were previously nationalized, but were privatized in the 1980s and 1990s. Maximum prices are now set by government regulatory bodies including OFWAT for water supply, OFTEL for telecommunications, and OFGEM for gas and electricity supply.

2 Brand reputation can sometimes help alleviate information problems. I might trust a brand that has a reputation for high quality, knowing that selling low-quality goods is unlikely to be in the firm's interests, since the long-term damage to its reputation is likely to outweigh any gains from a short-term increase in sales. This is a positive interpretation of branding. However, for other goods where quality is more subjective (such as fashion, cosmetics, or drinks), it is probably more accurate to regard a brand as having value because the firm has invested large amounts in advertising aimed at making us associate this brand with feeling happy, sexy, and attractive.

3 High income taxes may lead people to retire early, to avoid demanding and stressful jobs, or move to work in countries with lower taxes. Similarly, high rates of corporation tax can lead multinational firms to shift their operations (or at least their declared profits) to countries with lower taxes. A neat solution would be to tax things which the government wishes to discourage (such as the externalities associated with pollution or road congestion) rather than taxing working and making profits, which the government would like to encourage! However, in practice the scope for taxing such 'bads' is limited, and the sheer scale of total wages and profits means that the government has little choice but to tax these as well.

4 In Chapter 5 we see a similar problem when we consider whether the managers of firms can be assumed to be acting in the interests of their shareholders. For a more detailed discussion of government failure see Lipsey and Chrystal, *Economics* 14th edition, chapter 14.

5 The underlying problem here could be seen to lie in the property rights involved: I would be a fool to overuse a valuable resource that I own, but I have a strong incentive to overuse a resource that is collectively owned. For this reason, this problem has been termed 'the tragedy of the commons'. We return to the overuse of resources in Chapter 11. Also, see the case studies at the end of chapter 13 in Lipsey and Chrystal, *Economics* 14th edition.

6 For example, consider queue barging, talking during movies, or emissions of greenhouse gases (discussed in Chapter 11). Specifically, the prisoner's dilemma helps us understand the incentives which encourage people to impose externalities or to free ride in the funding of public goods.

Chapter 5

1 Unhappy shareholders have the power to sack such managers, but the job is complex, making it difficult to observe what the managers' real motives are. As a result, a large proportion of senior executive pay may be given in the form of share options or bonuses, rather than a fixed salary. This is intended to give managers exactly the same incentive as shareholders, motivating them to pursue policies which boost the company's share price. However, this may come with the unwanted side-effect of encouraging 'short-termism' as managers care strongly about policies which boost the share price in the short term, but not about the long term, after they are likely to have left the company.

2 For a more detailed discussion of the financial crisis and subsequent reform proposals see Lipsey and Chrystal, *Economics* 14th edition, chapter 12 (box 12.7 and the case studies) and the first case study in chapter 13. Some people argued that the crisis was evidence of a more general failure of capitalism, but this argument is by no means new (see Lipsey and Chrystal, *Economics* 14th edition, box 13.1), and the conclusion this time—as before—has been to try to reform markets so that they work better rather than abandon them in favour of central planning.

3 See Daniel Kahneman, *Thinking Fast and Slow* (Harmondsworth: Penguin, 2012). Professor Kahneman is a Nobel prize winner who has written an interesting and accessible book about his work. Also see Daniel Ariely, *Predictably Irrational* (New York: HarperCollins, 2008), and his TED talks.

4 For example 'In the US group 88% and in the Swedish group 77% believed themselves to be safer than the median driver.' Source: O. Svenson, 'Are we all less risky and more skillful than our fellow drivers?', *Acta Psychologica* 47.2 (1981), 143–8.

5 We would like to think that we read newspapers to gain objective information, but editors know us well, and are well aware that dramatic examples are more convincing than sober statistical analysis, and that they also need to offer us a political slant which is consistent with our existing views.

6 Men have been shown to be significantly more overconfident than women: M. A. Lundeberg, P. W. Fox, and J. Punćcohať, 'Highly confident but wrong: gender differences and similarities in confidence judgments', *Journal of Educational Psychology* 86.1 (1994), 114. Also, B. M. Barber and T. Odean, 'Boys will be boys: gender, overconfidence, and common stock investment', *Quarterly Journal of Economics* 116 (2001), 261–92.

7 The UK government set up the Behavioural Insights Team in 2010 to advise it on how to nudge us into actions such as eating better, saving for our retirements, or filling in our tax returns. See http://www.behaviouralinsights.co.uk.

8 If we mothball the plant, we might be lucky and find that it subsequently becomes profitable to operate (for example if uranium prices fall or electricity prices rise). But

this does not change the fact that it would be a mistake to operate the plant now. The government may also take into account the fact that this plant generates electricity without carbon dioxide emissions, unlike many other power sources. To keep this example simple, assume that this is already reflected in a higher price being paid for electricity which is not carbon-generated, so this externality will have been internalized into our profit projections.

Chapter 6

1 Government spending comprises two major components: (i) direct government expenditure on things like schools, roads, police, and defence; and (ii) transfer payments such as pensions and social security which give additional income to groups that are identified as being in particular need. We consider this redistributive role of government further in Chapter 11. Data: IMF WEO database.

Chapter 7

1 Economies are, of course, much more complex than this. After all, a car is much more than just a cleverly shaped piece of steel: it contains components from many different industries. Real supply chains are complex, and the double counting problem correspondingly more severe. However, we did not think that you would thank us for making Figure 7.3 any more complex than is needed to illustrate the underlying principle involved!

2 Investment goods (e.g. office buildings and factories) are used to help in the production of other goods, but unlike intermediate goods, they are not sold on to other firms. For this reason, investment spending is not double counted, so it should be included here. It should also, of course, increase the amount that the economy can produce in future.

3 It may seem odd that no allowance is made for the value of the ore extracted from the mine. After all, when calculating profits, companies deduct any rundown in stocks or depreciation of their assets. GDP is gross in the sense that no account is taken of these costs. This means that high GDP could be achieved by unsustainably running down natural resources, but a measure of gross economic activity is exactly what we need in order to explain booms and recessions. We consider sustainability in Chapter 11.

4 Putting these accounting definitions into practice inevitably raises some practical difficulties. In particular, the government charges indirect taxes on purchases of goods and services so the revenue received by firms for their produce is not the same as the amount paid by consumers. In the UK this amounts to 12.1% of GDP (mainly due to Value Added Tax), which must be added back into our calculation so that GDP calculated by each of our three methods gives the same answer.

5 One particular problem in distinguishing between real GDP growth and inflation is where the quality of goods changes. For example, computers have become much more powerful over time as well as cheaper, so measuring output simply as the number of computers produced would be misleading. For a more detailed discussion of GDP and the National Accounts see Lipsey and Chrystal, *Economics* 14th edition, chapter 15.

Chapter 8

1 For simplicity we will talk of a single wage. It would be more accurate to consider an index reflecting average wages in the whole economy. Assuming that all employees are the same and receive an identical wage is clearly simplistic, but is perfectly adequate to illustrate the underlying forces at work here. Note that in practice, there are also different ways of measuring unemployment: see Lipsey and Chrystal, *Economics* 14th edition, chapter 23 for details.

2 We can use conventional supply and demand analysis for a specific part of the labour market such as the market for painters and decorators, as we did in Chapter 5. If wages in this specific sector rise then more people might want to work as decorators (labour supply increases) and demand for their services might fall as some people choose DIY solutions instead (demand falls). As this is only a very small sector of the economy, shifts in wages do not have a big impact on total incomes in the economy. It is only when we consider the aggregate labour market (all employees in the economy) that the feedback loops in Figure 8.3 become so large that conventional supply and demand analysis becomes misleading.

3 Similarly, the 1929 stock market crash and the subsequent wave of bank failures in the USA were the catalyst which pushed the US economy—and the world economy as a whole—into the Great Depression of the 1930s. More generally, it may be surprising that even though saving for the future is encouraged as virtuous and prudent behaviour if, as in 2008, many consumers suddenly increase the proportion of their income that they save, this can pitch the whole economy into recession leaving everybody worse off. This is known as the *paradox of thrift*.

4 The Bank of England publishes a quarterly *Inflation Report* setting out its views on the prospects for future economic growth and inflation. The text goes into considerable detail, but just flicking through the charts can give a fairly clear picture of how the latest economic data have affected the Bank's judgement. The *Inflation Report* can be found at http://www.bankofengland.co.uk/publications/Pages/inflationreport/default.aspx.

5 In order to generate a significant stimulus the **fiscal deficit** (government spending in excess of total tax revenue) must be increased. A rise in government expenditure that is matched by a rise in taxation would have little net impact, since the increased injection is offset by an increased withdrawal. Several countries which were already running large deficits when the economy was booming (and hence had built up a large '**national debt**') found that the risk of becoming insolvent left them with limited scope for increased fiscal stimulus in the recession which followed the 2008 financial crisis. Effective fiscal policy depends on the government running only a modest deficit in good times so that it can increase borrowing in the bad times. For an extended discussion of cycles in the economy and the policies aimed at moderating them see Lipsey and Chrystal, *Economics* 14th edition, chapters 23 and 25.

Chapter 9

1 For an explanation of how a price index is constructed see the first case study at the end of chapter 15 of Lipsey and Chrystal, *Economics* 14th edition.

2 In such situations people might quite rightly conclude that the government would welcome higher inflation, since this would erode the real value of existing government debt, making it much easier to repay. This would be a short-sighted policy: the government gains in the short term, but in the longer term it suffers because, having been stung once, investors will subsequently demand much higher interest rates before they are willing to lend to the government. Nevertheless, desperate or cynical governments may wish to use inflation in this way.

3 Different definitions of the money supply have been used: the narrowest definition is just banknotes and coins in circulation; wider definitions include a range of different types of bank account. In the 1980s a succession of different definitions of the money supply were used as the government struggled to find a money supply target which behaved as they thought it would.

4 Like the demand curves we saw in Chapter 2, the AD curve slopes downwards, with higher prices leading to lower aggregate demand. This downward slope comes about because: (i) higher prices leave holders of some assets (such as cash or government bonds) worse off in real terms, lowering their consumer spending—Figure 9.2 showed an extreme example of this effect; (ii) higher aggregate prices in this country may leave its exports less competitive and imports more competitive (this is most likely where exchange rates are fixed, as they are between Eurozone countries; see Chapter 10).

5 This is the *short-run* AS curve. The economy can sustain an inflationary gap in the short term with only a modest rise in prices, but inflation is likely to keep rising as long as this gap is sustained, leading to an unlimited increase in prices in the long term. For this reason the long-run AS curve is vertical, consistent with inflation accelerating for as long as real GDP remains above the level implied by the NAIRU (see Box 9.2). The slope of the short-run AS curve used to be controversial. 'Keynesians' argued that it was fairly flat, so stimulatory fiscal and monetary policies would increase output without generating inflation. 'Neo-classical' economists argued instead that even in the short run the AS curve was near-vertical, so these demand side policies would just increase prices—instead 'supply side' policies were needed to increase output. Nowadays most economists regard the short-run AS curve as fairly flat at low levels of GDP (where economic resources are lying idle), but much steeper when the economy is operating near capacity.

6 Recent analysis finds that when analysing wages by region and occupational group 'the immigrant–native ratio has a statistically significant, small, negative impact' on wages. S. Nickell and J. Saleheen, 'The impact of immigration on occupational wages: evidence from Britain', Bank of England Staff Working Paper No. 574, December 2015. http://www.bankofengland.co.uk/research/Documents/workingpapers/2015/swp574.pdf.

Chapter 10

1 Interest and dividends on overseas assets owned by UK residents correspondingly reduce the deficit. The deficit is also corrected for transfers such as workers' remittances overseas and international aid flows.

2 Indeed, these global imbalances and the large international capital flows that they caused can be seen as contributing to the financial crisis of 2008. See case study 1 in chapter 24 of Lipsey and Chrystal, *Economics* 14th edition.

3 Restrictions on trade such as tariffs may be beneficial in some circumstances (e.g. as a temporary measure designed to allow a new industry to become competitive—the **infant industry argument**). But there are also several bogus arguments for such restrictions (see Lipsey and Chrystal, *Economics* 14th edition, chapter 27). There is also a severe danger of government failure in this area, for example if trade protection is adopted in response to lobbying by domestic producers who prefer not to have to compete with imports.

4 The same is true of international investment. For example, non-US investors wishing to buy shares in US companies such as Apple or Facebook first need to exchange some of their own currency for US dollars. Indeed, putting your savings into a wide range of different assets is very sensible *diversification* which reduces overall risk. A crash in the UK equity market might affect all UK shares. I could instead invest in equities in many different countries, bonds issued by many different borrowers, and perhaps also other assets such as real estate. The value of one or more of these different assets might collapse, but they are unlikely to all collapse.

5 This is known as a **depreciation** of the British pound, and a corresponding **appreciation** of the US dollar, for example if the exchange rate shifted from $1.50 per pound to $1.30. Each pound now buys fewer dollars than before, making it more expensive to import US goods into the UK. Conversely, US consumers can now buy more pounds with their dollars, making it cheaper for them to import from the UK. Don't worry if you find the way that these rates are quoted confusing—everyone does at first, since these are **relative prices** (the price of one currency in terms of another).

6 Exchange rate movements do not only shift export and import demand. They also have a direct impact on inflation since they make imports more or less expensive.

7 The exchange rates between most EU countries have now been fixed by abolishing the different national currencies and replacing them with the euro (the value of the euro is still allowed to fluctuate against other currencies). Whilst removing exchange rate volatility is welcome, this monetary union also means that monetary policy must now be set for the whole euro area by the ECB (European Central Bank). Previously, each country's central bank (France, Spain, Greece, etc.) could set interest rates at the level it thought appropriate for its own economy, but this is no longer possible. To see why, imagine that two central banks tried to set different interest rates within the same currency: no one would borrow at the higher of the two rates, and no one would lend at the lower.

Chapter 11

1 Real GDP growth has averaged 2% per annum over the period shown in Figure 11.1, gradually leading to an approximately fourteen-fold rise in real GDP. These figures cannot be precise since they depend on estimates of how the prices and quantities of goods produced in 1885 compare with the very different goods produced today. However, there can be no doubt that there has been a massive increase in material living standards over this period.

2 There has also been a significant increase in participation by women in paid employment (which is included in GDP) rather than housework (which is not). This process has been aided by technological improvements which allow domestic tasks to be achieved more rapidly, such as washing machines and fridges/freezers which allow prepared foods and less frequent

shopping (in some countries religious and cultural resistance to the education or employment of women has impeded this source of growth). Offsetting this increased participation by women, a larger proportion of the UK population is now in education or retirement.

3   We described long-term growth in GDP as entirely distinct from the short-term demand-led fluctuations we saw in Chapter 8. However, there are some potential links between the two. Individuals' job skills may tend to deteriorate or become outdated during a period of unemployment: in effect their human capital is seen as depreciating if it is not used and updated. Thus, high unemployment during a recession may have a persistent impact on **potential GDP**. Investment may also be deterred by fears of future economic volatility. Finally, some argue that booms and recessions are an inevitable part of the process by which new technology is adopted (installation of new technology leads to a boom, whilst old technology is scrapped during the subsequent recession). This view is particularly associated with economist Joseph Schumpeter, who termed this process '**creative destruction**', but other economists see no such innate link between technological change and recession.

4   For a discussion of the pros and cons of government intervention see Lipsey and Chrystal, *Economics* 14th edition, chapter 14.

5   The IMF maintains a very useful database which allows GDP growth (and many other economic data) to be compared across time and across different countries: World Economic Outlook, http://www.imf.org/external/data.htm.

6   See the World Bank poverty headcount ratio: http://data.worldbank.org/indicator/.

7   Such natural resources may even be a curse if they help finance conflict, lead to an appreciation of the currency which makes other exports uncompetitive, or lead to increased economic volatility due to shifts in global commodity prices. Climate may be another impediment in some cases—most of the poorest economies are in the tropics, with some endemic disease problems, but other tropical countries have become wealthy.

8   The World Bank produces **indicators** of government quality for different countries: http://info.worldbank.org/governance/wgi/index.aspx#home. A high degree of ethnic fragmentation within a country tends to be associated with lower-quality government and more frequent ethnic conflict.

9   UN World Population Prospects (2015 Revision): https://esa.un.org/unpd/wpp/. The 'green revolution' led to dramatic growth in agricultural yields per hectare in Asia, but in sub-Saharan Africa increased production has instead tended to be associated with increasing areas being dedicated to agriculture, resulting in greater environmental degradation. The challenge now is to raise agricultural productivity without further exacerbating this environmental damage. See J.-J. Dethier and A. Effenberger, 'Agriculture and development: a brief review of the literature', World Bank Policy Research Working Paper 5553 (2011).

10 The State of Food Insecurity in the World 2015 (UN): http://www.fao.org/3/a-i4671e.pdf.

11 For example, the deaths associated with the collectivization of agriculture in the Soviet Union in the 1930s, and the Chinese Great Leap Forward of 1958–62. More generally, see Dethier and Effenberger, 'Agriculture and development: a brief review of the literature' and A. Sen, *Poverty and Famines: An Essay on Entitlement and Deprivation* (Oxford: Oxford University Press, 1981).

12 See case study 2 in Lipsey and Chrystal, *Economics* 14th edition, chapter 26.

13 'Surface temperature is projected to rise over the 21st century under all assessed emission scenarios. It is very likely that heat waves will occur more often and last longer, and that extreme precipitation events will become more intense and frequent in many regions. The ocean will continue to warm and acidify, and global mean sea level to rise', Intergovernmental Panel on Climate Change, *Climate Change 2014: Synthesis Report*.

14 See case study 4 in chapter 10 of Lipsey and Chrystal, *Economics* 14th edition. For data covering many countries, see 'Income Inequality—The Gap between Rich and Poor', OECD (2015).

15 In case you are curious, in Figure 11.3 the UK is the point at GDP per capita of $39,000 and an average happiness of 6.8. For comparison, the USA also recorded average happiness of 6.8 in 2016, but an average GDP of $53,000. The full dataset can be found in the World Happiness Report 2017, chapter 2, online data, table 2.1 (http://worldhappiness.report/).

16 For a summary of the latest data and research see the World Happiness Report 2017, chapter 2, online data, table 2.1 (http://worldhappiness.report/); also Richard Layard, *Happiness: Lessons from a New Science* (Harmondsworth: Penguin, 2006).

17 Analysis of survey data suggests that spending money on other people has more impact on our happiness than spending money on ourselves: E. W. Dunn, L. B. Aknin, and M. I. Norton, 'Spending money on others promotes happiness', *Science* 319.5870 (2008), 1687–8. This has been confirmed by other studies such as an experiment which gave people cash and then asked them at random either to spend it on themselves or give it to a local charity. The second group showed a larger increase in happiness: L. B. Aknin, et al., 'Prosocial spending and well-being: cross-cultural evidence for a psychological universal', *Journal of Personality and Social Psychology* 104.4 (2013), 635–52.

GLOSSARY

absolute advantage The advantage that one region or person is said to have over another in the production of a given good when an equal quantity of resources can produce more of that good in the first region than in the second. Compare *comparative advantage*.

AD curve See *aggregate demand curve*.

adverse selection An example is the tendency for people most at risk to insure themselves, whilst people least at risk do not, so that the insurer gets a disproportionate number of high-risk clients. In general, it involves selection where quality is uncertain and care needs to be taken to avoid abnormally poor-quality goods or services.

agent Any person involved in economic decision-making.

aggregate demand (AD) The total desired purchases of the economy's final output at the current average price level.

aggregate demand curve A curve relating consumers' total desired output to the aggregate price level in the economy.

aggregate demand shock A shift in the *aggregate demand curve*, for example resulting from changes in consumer confidence or deliberate shifts in monetary or fiscal policy.

aggregate supply The total amount that will be produced and offered for sale at each aggregate price level.

aggregate supply curve A curve relating *aggregate supply* to the aggregate price level.

aggregate supply shock A shift in the *aggregate supply curve*, for example resulting from a shift in commodity prices or a technological change.

appreciation When a change in the *exchange rate* raises the value of the specified currency relative to others.

AS curve See *aggregate supply curve*.

asymmetric information A situation in which some economic agents have more information than others and this affects the outcome of a transaction between them.

at the margin Decisions taken at the margin are arrived at by considering whether a slight adjustment to the current situation would be an improvement. For example, firms can consider whether increasing (or decreasing) production by one unit would increase profits, and consumers can consider how much consuming one more unit of a particular product would increase their total utility.

balance of payments accounts A summary record of a country's transactions that involve payments and receipts of foreign exchange.

balance of trade The difference between the value of imports and exports of goods and services.

barriers to entry Anything that prevents new firms from entering an industry. These can be natural, such as substantial economies of scale, or created, such as a patent, or when firms engage in excessive advertising to make it difficult for a new firm to compete.

behavioural economics A field of economics which replaces simple assumed motives (in particular the assumption that consumers make rational choices designed to maximize their utility) with more complex motives and behaviours, often drawn from psychology.

black market A market in which goods are sold in violation of some legally imposed pricing or trading restriction.

bond A tradable debt contract carrying a legal obligation to pay interest and repay the principal at some stated future time.

budget deficit Usually refers to the *fiscal deficit* run by the government.

budget surplus Usually refers to the *fiscal surplus* run by the government.

cartel A group of firms that agree amongst themselves to cooperate rather than compete, raising prices in order to increase their total profits.

central bank A bank that acts as banker to the commercial banking system and often to the government as well. In the modern world it is usually a government-owned institution that is the sole money-issuing authority and has a key role in setting and implementing *monetary policy*. The UK central bank is the Bank of England.

central bank independence The policy of allowing the central bank to implement monetary policy without direct government control. Typically the government sets a target level for inflation, but leaves the central bank free to set interest rates at whatever level it deems necessary to meet this target. The key aim of central bank independence is to increase the credibility of monetary policy and hence reduce expected inflation. The central banks of most developed economies are now independent.

centrally planned economy An economy in which the decisions of the government (as distinct from households and firms) exert the major influence over the allocation of resources and the distribution of income. Also called a command economy.

classical economics A term loosely used to refer to all mainstream economics up to the 1950s. This body of theory was criticized by Keynes.

comparative advantage The ability of one nation (or region or individual) to produce a good or service at a lower opportunity cost in terms of other products forgone than another nation (or region or individual). Compare *absolute advantage*.

competition policy Policy designed to prohibit the acquisition and exercise of excessive market power by firms. It is designed to prevent monopolies from arising, or abusing their power where they do exist, and also to prohibit non-competitive behaviour by oligopolistic firms.

complementary goods (complements) Two goods for which the quantity demanded of one is negatively related to the price of the other, typically because they need to be used together to meet one underlying need (e.g. cars and petrol

are of little use separately, but together provide transport).

consumer price index (CPI) An index of the general price level based on the consumption pattern of typical consumers.

consumer surplus The difference between the value that consumers place on the total amount of a good or service that they consume, and the payment they must make to purchase this amount. The difference between what consumers actually pay and the maximum they would be willing to pay for this amount.

cost-push inflation The tendency for prices to rise throughout the economy as producers raise the prices of their products in order to protect their profit margins following an increase in raw material prices.

creative destruction Schumpeter's theory that high profits and wages earned by monopolistic or oligopolistic firms are the spur for others to invent cheaper or better substitute products and techniques that allow their suppliers to gain some of these profits thus eroding the previously existing market power.

credibility The extent to which agents in the private sector of the economy believe that the government will carry out the policy it promises. This is important because expectations of future government policy action can influence current behaviour.

credit crunch A general collapse of lending in which even borrowers who were previously considered reliable now find it impossible to borrow.

current account deficit When all international transactions between one country and the rest of the world related to goods and services, income payments, and receipts are totalled, a current account deficit is recorded if the payments exceed the receipts. The largest single component of the UK current account deficit has tended to be its *trade deficit*, as the value of imports into the UK exceeds the value of exports from it.

demand The amount of a good or service that an individual or group would be willing to buy at a specified price.

demand curve A graphical relation showing the quantity of some good or service that households would like to buy at each possible price.

demand management See *demand side policies.*

demand-pull inflation The tendency for the general price level to rise when the economy is booming, typically because employees demand wage rises or producers attempt to increase their profit margins.

demand shock A change in demand for a good (or service) which results from something other than a change in the price of this product (e.g. a reduction in incomes or a change in the price of a substitute good). This change shifts the demand curve for the product.

demand side policies Policies designed to reduce unemployment by boosting demand. These include *fiscal policy, monetary policy,* and *quantitative easing.*

depreciation (1) The loss in value of an asset over time due to physical wear and tear and obsolescence. (2) A shift in the free-market exchange rate which reduces the value of the specified currency in terms of other currencies.

developed economies Usually refers to the rich industrial economies of North America, Western Europe, Japan, and Australasia.

developing countries The lower-income countries of the world, most of which are in Asia, Africa, and South and Central America. Also called emerging economies.

development economics The study of poorer (less-developed) economies, aiming in particular to identify the reasons why they have so far failed to catch up with more developed economies.

diminishing marginal utility The observation that the satisfaction (utility) that a consumer gains from consuming one more unit of a good or service tends to decline as the amount consumed increases. For example, I am likely to enjoy eating my first ice cream today more than my second, and far more than my twentieth!

economies of scale A situation in which unit costs fall as output increases, enabling large firms to produce at lower unit costs than small firms.

efficiency wage A wage rate above the market-clearing level that enables employers to attract the best workers as well as to provide their employees with an incentive to perform well so as to avoid being sacked.

elastic Where the percentage change in the quantity demanded or supplied is greater than the percentage change in the factor that caused it. This corresponds to a price or income elasticity greater than 1 in absolute value.

elasticity of demand See *price elasticity of demand.*

elasticity of supply See *price elasticity of supply.*

EMU (Economic and Monetary Union) Adoption by EU countries of a common currency (the euro) in place of their previous separate currencies.

equities Certificates (or electronic records) indicating part ownership of a joint-stock company. Also known as shares.

ERM (Exchange Rate Mechanism) System which attempted to keep exchange rates between European Union countries stable. Most currencies in the ERM have now joined *EMU* instead.

excess demand The amount by which the quantity demanded exceeds the quantity supplied at a given price; negative *excess supply.*

excess supply The amount by which the quantity supplied exceeds the quantity demanded at a given price; negative *excess demand.*

exchange rate The price at which two national currencies can be exchanged for each other. The amount of one currency needed to buy one unit of the other currency.

externality A cost or benefit of a transaction that falls on agents not involved in the decision (e.g the effects of pollution on third parties).

final goods and services The outputs of the economy after eliminating all double counting, i.e. excluding all intermediate goods.

fiscal deficit A shortfall of current government revenue below current expenditure.

fiscal policy Policy designed to influence aggregate demand by altering government spending and/or taxes, thereby shifting the *AD curve.*

fiscal surplus The amount by which current government revenue exceeds current expenditure.

fixed exchange rate An exchange rate that is held within a narrow range around some pre-announced value. Typically the country's central bank intervenes by buying/selling its currency in the foreign-exchange market in order to keep it within the desired range.

floating exchange rate An exchange rate that is left free to be determined on the foreign-exchange market by the forces of demand and supply.

foreign exchange (FX) market The market where currencies are traded—at prices that are expressed by the *exchange rate*.

framing The exact way in which a problem is presented, or a question is asked. Studies in psychology and behavioural economics have demonstrated that people may make very different choices in a given situation, depending on exactly how the choices are presented.

free riding The problem that arises because people have a self-interest in not paying for a *public good* in the hope that others will pay for it.

free trade The absence of any form of government interference with the free flow of international trade.

game theory The study of *strategic* choices, applicable when the outcome for one person depends on the behaviour of others.

GDP See *gross domestic product*.

GDP gap The difference between actual GDP and potential GDP. Also called the output gap. Negative output gaps are sometimes called recessionary gaps; positive output gaps are sometimes called inflationary gaps.

globalization The increased worldwide interdependence of most economies. Integrated financial markets, the sourcing of components throughout the world, the growing importance of transnational firms, and the linking of many service activities through the new information and communications technologies are some of its many manifestations.

goods Tangible products, such as cars or shoes. Sometimes all goods and services are loosely referred to as goods.

government failure Where flawed government intervention imposes costs that would have been avoided if it had acted differently.

gross domestic product (GDP) The value of total output actually produced in the whole economy over some period (usually a year, although quarterly data are also available). Nominal GDP is in current money terms. Real GDP is a volume measure that removes the effects of inflation.

groupthink A term from behavioural economics referring to our tendency to hold the same opinions as those around us.

household All people living under one roof and taking joint financial decisions.

human capital The capitalized value of the productive capabilities of a person. Usually refers to value derived from expenditures on education, training, and health improvements.

hyperinflation Episodes of very rapid inflation.

implicit contract Details of what employee and employer can expect from each other (such as the scope for future promotion and pay rises) which, although important, are not included in the formal contract signed by these two parties.

income elasticity (of demand) The responsiveness of quantity demanded to a change in income. Measured as the percentage change in quantity demanded divided by the percentage change in income that brought about this change.

indicators Data that investors and policy-makers monitor for information about the state of the economy.

inelastic When the percentage change in quantity is less than the percentage change in price or income that brought it about (i.e. elasticity is less than 1 in absolute value).

infant-industry argument The argument that new domestic industries with potential economies of scale need to be protected from competition from established low-cost foreign producers so that they can grow large enough to achieve costs as low as those of foreign producers.

inferior good A good with a negative *income elasticity*, implying that demand for it diminishes when income increases. Compare *normal good*.

inflation A positive rate of increase in the general price level in the economy.

injections Additional spending flows which increase the circular flow of income between domestic households and firms. In a simple macro model the injections are government spending, exports, and investment.

interest rate The percentage of the amount borrowed which must be paid each year as interest on the loan.

intermediate goods and services (intermediates) All goods and services which, rather than being consumed directly, are used as inputs into the production of other goods and services.

internalizing the externality A policy which gives decision-makers an incentive to take account of the *externalities* that they cause and take appropriate steps to reduce them (assuming that these externalities are harmful). Examples are carbon taxes and congestion charging.

investment The act of producing or purchasing goods that are not for immediate consumption. These are durable goods that will form part of the physical capital stock, housing, and additions to inventories of goods.

Keynesian revolution The adoption of the idea (first proposed by J. M. Keynes) that the government can use monetary and fiscal policy to control aggregate demand and thereby influence the level of GDP and unemployment.

labour force See *workforce*.

long run A period of time over which all inputs used by a firm may be varied but the basic technology of production is unchanged.

long-run aggregate supply curve A curve that relates the aggregate price level to equilibrium real GDP after all input costs, including wage rates, have been fully adjusted to eliminate any excess demand or supply.

marginal cost The increase in a firm's total costs as a result of raising the rate of production by one unit.

marginal revenue The change in total revenue resulting from selling one extra unit per period of time.

marginal utility The change in satisfaction resulting from consuming one more unit of a good or service.

market An area in either geographical or cyberspace in which buyers and sellers negotiate the exchange of a specified product.

market economy A society in which people meet most of their material wants through exchanges voluntarily agreed upon by the contracting parties, with limited intervention by the government. Often referred to as a free market economy.

market failure Any market performance that is less than the most efficient possible (the optimal) performance. Key reasons for market failure are natural monopoly, information problems, externalities, and public goods.

market structure The characteristics of a market that influence the behaviour and performance of firms that sell in the market. The four main market structures are *perfect competition, monopolistic competition, oligopoly,* and *monopoly.*

monetarism The theory that the money supply exerts a powerful influence over the economy and that control of the money supply is a potent means of affecting the economy's macroeconomic behaviour.

monetary policy Policy of seeking to control aggregate demand, and ultimately GDP and the inflation rate, by adjusting short-term interest rates, and more recently, by *quantitative easing*.

money supply The total amount of money circulating in the economy. Also called the supply of money or the money stock.

monopolist The sole seller of a product or service.

monopolistic competition A market structure in which there are many sellers and new firms are able to enter the industry, but in which each firm sells a slightly different version of the product and, as a result, faces a negatively sloped demand curve for its own product.

monopoly A market structure in which the industry contains only one producer.

moral hazard The change in behaviour which results from people being protected against risk, for example, starting to drive more carelessly when they have accident insurance.

multiplier The ratio of the change in GDP to the size of the change (e.g. a tax cut) which brought it about.

NAIRU The Non-Accelerating-Inflation Rate of Unemployment'. The level of unemployment that is consistent with a constant rate of inflation.

national debt The total debt of the central government, arising as a result of previous *fiscal deficits.*

natural monopoly An industry for which a single producer is clearly more efficient than having competing firms, typically because of large *economies of scale.*

negative sum game An interaction in which some participants win and others lose, but in which the total losses made by the losers exceed the gains made by the winners. See also *positive sum game, zero sum game.*

net exports Total exports of goods and services minus total imports.

nominal GDP Total output of the economy valued at current prices. This can rise due to either real GDP growth or inflation. Also known as 'money GDP'.

normal good A good or service for which demand increases when income increases. Compare *inferior good*.

oligopoly An industry that contains only a few firms that interact strategically. The outcome for each is affected by what the others do.

OPEC Organization of Petroleum Exporting Countries, a permanent, intergovernmental organization to regulate petroleum production, created in 1960.

opportunity cost Measurement of the cost of one choice in terms of the value of the alternatives forgone.

perfectly competitive industry (perfect competition) A market structure in which there is a large number of firms in an industry, more are free to enter, and all produce goods which consumers regard as identical. This extremely competitive environment means that each individual firm must sell at the same price as its competitors (setting a higher price would generate no sales, and a lower price is likely to be loss-making). Thus the demand curve for each individual firm appears flat, even though the demand curve for the industry as a whole slopes down.

positive sum game An interaction in which some participants win and others lose, but in which the total gains made by the winners exceed the total losses made by the losers. See also *negative sum game, zero sum game*.

potential GDP (potential output) The level of GDP which is consistent with unemployment being at the NAIRU, implying that inflation is stable—neither rising nor falling.

price discrimination Situation arising when firms sell different units of their output at different prices for reasons not associated with differences in costs.

price elasticity of demand The percentage change in quantity demanded divided by the percentage change in price that caused it. Usually just called elasticity of demand.

price elasticity of supply The percentage change in quantity supplied divided by the percentage change in price that caused it. Usually just called elasticity of supply.

private sector That portion of an economy in which production is owned and operated by private (non-government) bodies. Compare *public sector*.

production possibility boundary A curve that shows the alternative combinations of goods and services that can just be produced if all available productive resources in the economy are fully employed and used efficiently; the boundary between attainable and unattainable output combinations (see Figure 2.10).

progressive tax A system which charges richer people a higher proportion of their incomes as tax.

public goods Goods and services that, once produced, can be consumed by everyone, such as police protection and parks. Also called collective consumption goods.

public sector That portion of an economy in which production is owned and operated by the government or by bodies created and controlled by it, such as nationalized industries. Compare *private sector*.

quantitative easing The purchase of government and corporate bonds by the *central bank* on a large scale intended to raise the money supply, influence asset prices, and affect long-term interest rates. This policy has been used by central banks which wanted to stimulate *aggregate demand* but could not lower interest rates any further.

real GDP Total economic output valued at prices from a specified base year, for example, GDP at 1999 prices. It is a volume measure of real economic activity that removes the effects of inflation.

recession A sustained drop in the level of aggregate economic activity, officially defined to occur when real GDP drops for two successive quarters.

regret The emotional pain associated with realizing that we have made a bad decision. Studies in psychology and behavioural economics have found that this can have a substantial impact on our decision-making.

relative price Any price expressed as a ratio of another price or price index.

scarce A resource is considered scarce if using more of it for one purpose necessitates using less of it for another purpose. By contrast, we can use more of a plentiful resource for a new purpose whilst continuing to use it as before for existing purposes.

services Intangible rather than physical products, for example, haircuts and medical services.

shares See *equities*.

short run The period of time over which firms cannot adjust some of their inputs, such as physical capital.

specialization When applied to countries, it refers to producing in the domestic economy products for which the country has a *comparative advantage* and importing those for which it has a comparative disadvantage. When applied to labour within a country, it refers to specialization in particular tasks rather than each person producing a wide range of products.

stagflation The simultaneous occurrence of a positive GDP gap (with its accompanying high unemployment) and rising inflation.

stock exchange The market in which investors can buy or sell *shares*. Most shares are now traded electronically.

strategic behaviour Decisions that take into account the reactions of others to one's own actions, e.g. when an oligopolistic firm takes into account how its competitors might react to a price cut.

substitute Two goods are substitutes if the quantity demanded of one is positively related to the price of the other, typically because they are alternative means of meeting an underlying need (e.g. train and air travel).

sunk costs Costs already committed to a project which cannot be recovered even if the project is now abandoned.

supply The amount of a good or service that an individual or group would be willing to sell at a specified price.

supply curve The graphical representation of the relation between the quantity of some good or service that producers wish to make and sell per period of time and its price, other relevant factors remaining unchanged.

supply shock A change in the supply of a good (or service) which results from something other than a change in the price of this product. This change shifts the supply curve for the product.

supply-side policies Policies that seek to shift the *aggregate supply curve* to the right, by increasing the productive efficiency of the economy. Examples are policies aimed at equipping the workforce with skills that are currently in short supply, and policies aimed at increasing entrepreneurship or the degree of competition between firms.

systemic risk The risk of widespread financial disruption if the collapse of one financial institution leads to the collapse of others in a chain reaction.

tacit collusion When firms arrive at a cooperative solution (which increases their joint profit) even though they have not explicitly agreed to cooperate.

trade deficit Occurs when the value of exports from the economy is less than the value of imports into it.

trade union A union covering workers with a common set of skills, no matter where, or for whom, they work.

utility The total satisfaction derived from consuming some amount of a good or service.

value added The value of a firm's output minus the value of the inputs that it purchases from other firms.

very long run A period of time over which the technological possibilities open to a firm or the economy as a whole are subject to change.

visible trade Trade in physical products. Sometimes called merchandise trade.

visibles Tangible goods such as cars, aluminium, coffee, and iron ore, which we can see when traded across international borders.

wage–price spiral The tendency for inflation to remain high even after the conditions that initially caused it have passed. Employees may continue to demand wage rises to compensate for the effect of previous price rises (thus protecting their real wage), whilst employers continue to raise prices in order to pass on their increased wage bills.

withdrawals Spending that leaves the domestic economy and does not create further incomes for domestic residents. Import spending, for example, creates incomes overseas. Also called leakages. The main withdrawals from the circular flow between households and firms are savings, taxes, and imports.

workforce The total of the employed, the self-employed, and the unemployed, i.e. those of working age who have a job plus those who are looking for work.

zero sum game An interaction in which some participants win and others lose, but in which the total gains made by the winners exactly balance the total losses made by the losers. See also *negative sum game, positive sum game*.

INDEX

Introductory Note

References such as '178–9' indicate (not necessarily continuous) discussion of a topic across a range of pages. Wherever possible in the case of topics with many references, these have either been divided into sub-topics or only the most significant discussions of the topic are listed. Because the entire work is about 'economics', the use of this term (and certain others which occur constantly throughout the book) as an entry point has been restricted. Information will be found under the corresponding detailed topics.

L

labour 4, 16, 41, 43–4, 46, 63–5, 78, 87
labour force, *see* workforce
labour markets 43–4, 46, 48, 50–1, 54, 63, 65, 67
  aggregate 65, 97, 106
  incentive problems 44–6
laissez-faire 97
lenders 46–7, 82
living standards 2, 61–2, 69, 87, 89, 91, 93, 95
loans 46–7, 82, 90, 114
  housing 47–8
  student 46
long run 102, 115, 117
long-term growth 56, 79, 87, 93, 95, 109
lump of labour fallacy 78
luxuries 8, 99

M

macroeconomic policy 46, 57, 84, 97–8
macroeconomics, definition 4
Malthus, Thomas 90
managers 27, 36, 45, 50, 103–4
manufacturers 8, 11, 14, 30, 57–9
marginal costs 22–4, 28, 115
marginal revenue 22–4, 28, 115
marginal utility 20–3, 27, 94, 113, 115
  diminishing 20, 94, 113
market-clearing wage 44–5
market dynamics 11–13
market economy (free market economy) 2, 4, 29, 43, 53, 115
market failure 28–41, 53–4, 99, 115
  asymmetric information 35
  externalities 31–4
  information problems 30–2, 34
  natural monopolies 29, 34
  public goods 33–6, 41, 53, 104, 115–16
market structures 27, 115–16
markets 2, 4–5, 12–15, 17, 21–3, 43–4, 46–7, 114–15
  black 111
  financial 4, 41, 114
  foreign-exchange 83–4, 113
  free 13, 30, 41, 92, 99
  insurance 35
  labour, *see* labour markets
  response to shocks 14–17

microeconomics, definition 4
migrant workers 78
minimum wages 46
models 6, 27, 30, 50, 53–4, 95, 99, 102
  classical 97, 99
  Keynesian 66, 97, 99
monetarism 73, 97, 115
monetary policy 67–8, 73–5, 77–9, 84–5, 87, 97–8, 107–8, 112–13
  definition 115
monetary union 108, 113
money supply 78–9, 107, 115–16
  growth 72–3
  and inflation 72–4
  targets 73, 78, 107
monopolistic competition 26–7, 115
monopolist 22, 24–5, 27–8, 33, 115
monopoly 21–3, 24, 26–9, 34, 54, 102–3, 112, 115
  natural 29, 34, 41, 53, 115
moral hazard 35, 115
motives/motivations 35, 39, 44–5, 48, 76, 104, 111
multiplier 67, 115

N

NAIRU (Non-Accelerating Inflation Rate of Unemployment) 75–8, 107, 115–16
national debt 106, 115
natural monopolies 34, 41, 53, 115
  and market failure 29
natural resources 2, 16, 83, 87, 89, 105, 109
negative sum games 22–3, 115–16, 118
net exports 85, 116
new equilibrium 14, 17, 75–6
new firms 26–7, 111, 115
noise pollution 31
Non-Accelerating Inflation Rate of Unemployment, *see* NAIRU
normal goods 114, 116
North Korea 2
nudging 41, 50, 104

O

oil 11, 14, 40, 89, 101
  prices 40, 70–1, 76, 79
oligopoly 27, 112, 115–17
OPEC (Organization of the Petroleum Exporting Countries) 40, 116
opportunity cost 16–17, 82–3, 112, 116

Organization of the Petroleum Exporting Countries, *see* OPEC
outcomes 13, 31, 36–7, 39–40, 111, 114, 116
  cooperative 39–40
  uncooperative 38
  undesirable 29, 38, 41, 53
output 16–17, 40, 74, 76–7, 102, 107, 113, 116
  gap (GDP gap) 58, 116
overconfidence, *see* confidence
overfishing 38–9, 92
overseas assets 82, 107

P

paradox of thrift 106
patents 103, 111
pensions 46, 49, 105
perfect competition 24, 26–8, 115–16
planned economies 2, 13, 17, 29, 112
politicians 50, 78–9, 85, 97, 99
pollution 31, 38, 91, 103, 113
population growth 90–1, 95
positive demand shock 9, 11, 15, 17, 75, 78
positive sum games 23, 83, 115–16, 118
potential GDP (gross domestic product) 57, 109, 116
poverty 89–91, 95, 98, 109
price discrimination 25, 28, 54, 116
price elasticity 7–8, 101
  of demand 113, 116
  of supply 113, 116
price level 75–6, 111–15, 117
prices
  maximum 29, 103
  raw materials 11, 14, 112
  relative 108, 117
prisoner's dilemma 36, 38–41, 54, 91, 95, 104
private sector 16–17, 82, 97, 112, 116
producers 2, 4, 10, 12–13, 19–30, 111–13, 115, 117
production 10–12, 22, 24, 63–4, 102, 105, 111, 114–16
  possibility boundary 116
  processes 16, 31, 87, 102
productive capacity 74, 82
productivity 83, 87, 109
products 5–6, 8, 16–17, 19–20, 26–7, 101–3, 112–15, 117
  identical 24, 26–7
profit margin 10–11, 70–1, 102, 112–13